C000226794

HISTORY OF
MEN'S FASHION

HISTORY OF MEN'S FASHION

What the Well-Dressed Man is Wearing

by
Nicholas Storey

REMEMBER WHEN

To the memory of my sister
SARA MARGARET STOREY
1962–2005

and to our parents
JOHN STEWART STOREY AND LILIAN EDITH JOYCE STOREY
for
his sense of exactitude
her sense of romance
and
for both continuing to expect something
are these pages dedicated, with enduring love and affection

First published in Great Britain in 2008 and reprinted in 2010 by
Remember When
An imprint of
Pen & Sword Books Ltd
47 Church Street
Barnsley
South Yorkshire
S70 2AS

Copyright © Nicholas Storey, 2008, 2010

ISBN 978 1 84468 037 5

The right of Nicholas Storey to be identified as Author of this work has been
asserted by him in accordance with the Copyright, Designs and Patents Act 1988.

A CIP catalogue record for this book is
available from the British Library

All rights reserved. No part of this book may be reproduced or transmitted in any form
or by any means, electronic or mechanical including photocopying, recording or by any
information storage and retrieval system, without permission
from the Publisher in writing.

Printed and bound in England
By CPI UK

Pen & Sword Books Ltd incorporates the Imprints of Pen & Sword Aviation,
Pen & Sword Family History, Pen & Sword Maritime, Pen & Sword Military, Wharncliffe
Local History, Pen & Sword Select, Pen & Sword Military Classics,
Leo Cooper, Remember When, Seaforth Publishing and Frontline Publishing

For a complete list of Pen & Sword titles please contact
PEN & SWORD BOOKS LIMITED
47 Church Street, Barnsley, South Yorkshire, S70 2AS, England
E-mail: enquiries@pen-and-sword.co.uk
Website: www.pen-and-sword.co.uk

Contents

Introduction

I remember that Lord Byron once described him to me, as having nothing remarkable in his style of dress, except a certain 'exquisite propriety'. (Leigh Hunt on Beau Brummell, quoted in Captain William Jesse, *The Life of George Brummell, Esq., Commonly called Beau Brummell*, 1844).

GEORGE Bryan Brummell (1778–1840) was a sometime friend of, and sartorial adviser to, the Prince Regent. He is described on the blue plaque on his former house at 4 Chesterfield Street, Mayfair, as 'Leader of Fashion' and is widely recognized as a leading influence in the rise in importance of Savile Row as a centre of excellence for men's tailoring. He fled to France on 16 May 1816 (after dining on a cold fowl and a bottle of claret and going to the opera as usual), to escape his creditors after amassing gambling debts. If anything Brummell's fame in life has been surpassed by the legend and stories still told of his elegance and wit.

George Gordon, Lord Byron (1788–1824), was a great Scottish romantic poet and international rascal.

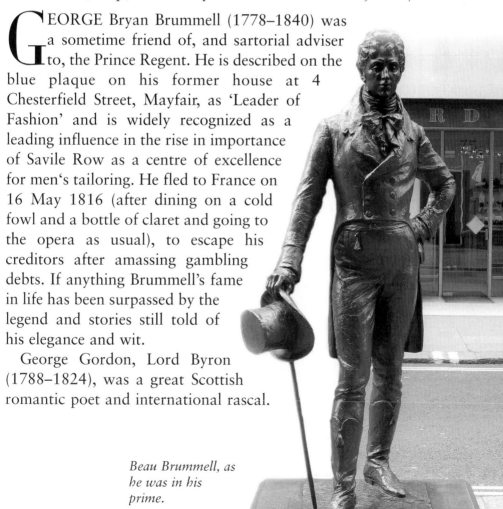

Beau Brummell, as he was in his prime.

It was said that Byron always spoke Brummell's name with a 'mixture of jealousy and awe' and rated him with the victor of Waterloo, the Duke of Wellington, as 'the greatest men of the age'.

Anyone who thinks that he is going everywhere (or even *anywhere*) should have, as a *minimum*, the selection of apparel described in this book and realize that if you want to get ahead you need to get a hat – but not just any old hat will do. Moreover, especially bearing in mind that many quotations from other works, in books of all kinds, seldom have anything but amusement value or are merely to show that the author has a thick dictionary of popular quotations at hand, I would urge my reader strictly to apply the essential truths to be found in the quotations in this work in every aspect of personal adornment. In short, when in doubt (over, say, the advisability of purple socks, straw hats in Town or white mess jackets with gold buttons), ask: what would Jeeves have said?

Beau Brummell's 'exquisite propriety' was the reverse of foppery – which is generally (mistakenly) associated even now with Brummell's name. There was nothing remarkable about his dress except that it was modest, subdued and most proper to the occasion and of the best materials and making. Strictly, he was a Dandy and certainly not a Popinjay. That he did describe himself as a 'Dandy' is clear from the fact that he joined with three of his friends to give the Dandies' Ball in the Argyle Rooms in July 1813, to celebrate their recent gambling wins. The Argyle Rooms were fashionable entertainment rooms on the site of what is now Liberty's department store, in Argyle Street, off Regent Street.

The friends were William, Lord Alvanley (1789–1849), Sir Henry Mildmay Bt (1787–1848) and Henry Pierrepont. It was at the Dandies' Ball that, having been conspicuously snubbed by the Prince Regent, Brummell turned and said in a loud, clear voice to the Regent's departing back: 'Alvanley, who's your fat friend?' The mortification was not wholly forgiven until George IV's deathbed when, according to Ian Kelly's biography of Brummell (*Beau Brummell*, Sceptre, 2005), one of his last acts was apparently to abandon the feud and to grant Brummell a sinecure in France.

Brummell's dress derived in some measure from military patterns, cloths and colours (he had held a commission in the 10th Hussars 'The Prince of Wales' Own' cavalry regiment). One of his aphorisms was that the severest mortification a gentleman could incur was to attract observation in the street by his outward appearance – even though Captain Jesse also tells us that his *deportment* was so striking that, in walking down St James's Street, he attracted as much attention of the passers-by as the Prince of Wales himself. In short, he looked like *somebody*.

The Cornish writer, anthologist and academic Sir Arthur Quiller-Couch ('Q') (now chiefly remembered for compiling the *Oxford Book of English Verse*) laid no claim to dandyism of any kind; yet he was remarkable for his dress and the bright colours and checks which he employed; indeed, mention was made of this in an alphabetical rhyme at Cambridge when he was King Edward VII Professor of English literature there:

Q is for Q, in the late Verrall's boots;
His bedder plays draughts on his cast away suits.

(Dr A.W. Verrall was Q's immediate predecessor in the chair.) There is a great deal in his dictum that 'The trousers make the gentleman', because they are, indeed, of the utmost importance and often overlooked. The overall effect which he unintentionally achieved was to impress such as the author of *The Wind in the Willows* (and sometime secretary of the Bank of England) Kenneth Grahame and his young son, Alistair: 'the same Q looking not a day older and even more beautifully dressed than formerly' (see Brittain's biography for more details).

Montesquieu's famous maxim on taste 'Le goût est un je ne sais quoi' (literally: 'Taste is an I don't know what') is, at once, laconic and telling: we all instinctively know what he meant, even if we cannot all lay claim to the possession of taste or to its habitual and invariable application. I mean, as I sit and write this, my clothing demonstrates nothing less than the yearning of the moth for the star – tatty jumper and rather worn slippers.

Professor J.A.C. Thomas, Professor of Roman Law at University College London, was known for mismatching suits, loose, bright bow ties and scuffed Dr Martens' boots and he appeared and vanished in a cloud which seemed, at the time, to comprise equal quantities of profound but recondite learning and Wilson's snuff. However, in his *Textbook of Roman Law* (1976) he sums up the antiquity, the force and the effect of dress codes for us:

> In the *Corpus Iuris Civilis* (the body of civil law), it is clear, *ius non scriptum* (unwritten law) signifies custom. Here again it is necessary to particularize what is meant by custom. In modern society, there are practices and conventions which are generally observed though they have no legal, only a social, sanction – there are, for example, many men who think nothing of income tax avoidance but who would rather be seen dead than attend, in other than evening dress with white tie, a function at which ladies were present.

The example given in this statement is no longer true. It was not even true when it was written in 1976. The decline started during the First World War. However, the statement was true within the living memory of some. There is still (just) a social code, a custom, with social sanctions for disobedience to rules such as rules of dress: this code is now, over 30 years after Professor Thomas wrote, fading fast and, with every act of acquiescence to breaches of the code, we show up one aspect of our civilization as falling into a positively Roman decline.

The extent of the decline is emphasized by the fact that now events requiring even basic 'white tie' are virtually unknown and black tie requirements are going the same way. The enormously complicated variations in dress at court, as described for all categories of members of the royal household, officers in the navy and military and officials (with further variations, depending on the different occasions), were described in G.A. Titman's *Dress and Insignia Worn at His Majesty's Court* (1937). Since the Second World War the practice of such codes has, nearly entirely, been lost. Being lost with these codes are many of the group identities and even the sense of nationhood which they reinforced. With the loss of these things, social loyalties and convictions, the sense of duty and true patriotism diminish.

We should note and draw a lesson from the fact that the complex head-dresses and arrangements of animal skins of African warriors, specific to tribes, have a real social and military purpose and value and are not vain fripperies.

The Prince of Wales wore the dinner jacket version of Windsor Uniform at the announcement of his engagement to the then Mrs Parker-Bowles. But how many would recognize the scarlet collar and cuffs and special gilt buttons on his dark blue dinner jacket as the derivatives of the Windsor Uniform style of dress for male members of the Royal Household? This uniform reverses the colours of Royal Livery – which has red coats with blue trimmings – and was introduced by George III.

Indeed, now we have modern 'celebrities' pitching up to receive official honours in open-necked shirts. Less than 50 years ago people so dressed would not have got through the outer gates – let alone into the royal presence. I am unconvinced that we are a better society for the fact that we are quite so tolerant now; whether in relation to just this sort of thing – or even more important declines in standards, of which this is merely symptomatic.

In *The Angel in the Mist* Robert Speaight had a character express the opinion that 'Lobb and Lock . . . are the last luxuries of noble minds' - which amply demonstrates with what a deadly serious business we are primarily concerned. It is interesting to note too that these businesses (**John Lobb** and **James Lock**) have survived in the modern world (Lock's was established '*not later* than 1676') because, come hell or high water, there will always be a demand for the very best of everything.

I am not a style consultant or a colour coordinator; if you have invested in this book, the chances are that you have at least a moderately good idea of what colours and styles suit you and, if you fear that you do not, the shops and purveyors described will help you. That is their job. My task is to lead you to them.

Most of the items described in this book may reliably be bought from any of the several obvious makers and suppliers of such goods (bespoke and ready-made) in the magic quadrangle, centred on

*A feather in every cap: Sir Philip Mitchell, Governor-General of Kenya, and African chiefs awaiting the arrival, in 1952, at Nairobi airport, of the princess who would leave Africa as Queen Elizabeth II. The Governor-General is in his tropical uniform: photograph by Dmitri Kessel (*Time and Life Pictures Collection Getty Images)

Piccadilly and represented by Savile Row on the north, Bond Street and St James's Street on the west, Pall Mall on the south and Regent Street on the east (quite possibly the original 'gods' quad'). The name 'Piccadilly' derives from a type of high collar once sold in the Strand by a haberdasher called Robert Baker, who started the development of the land around what became Piccadilly Circus. Just spend a lazy afternoon walking around the area and look at the shops.

In Jermyn Street, outside the southern entrance to the Piccadilly Arcade, is the fairly recent (and superbly evocative) statue of Beau Brummell himself by the sculptress Irena Sedlecka. The cost was raised by subscription.

Generally, there is consistency of quality and price. However, in one or two instances, there are certain makers and suppliers which I believe are head and shoulders above the rest and these I mention in due course. Naturally, this is my personal choice and I mean no pejorative inference to be drawn against 'the rest'.

There are also makers and suppliers of broadly similar quality outside this quadrangle but finding them at all and then finding them consistent in their goods is another matter. However, they can, by virtue of lower overheads, represent true value for money; snip for snip and stitch for stitch. One such excellent place, for quality, consistency, price and overall value for money, is tailors **Connock & Lockie** in Lamb's Conduit Street, WC1. There is also **Timothy Everest** in Spitalfields – who brings a noteworthy contemporary twist to his work and who was acknowledged, and patronized, by the late John Morgan (who wrote for *GQ* magazine and the 'Modern Manners' column in *The Times* until his untimely death).

Ede & Ravenscroft, Hackett, Gieves & Hawkes and **Oliver Brown** are all excellent general outfitters who also supply ready-made most items of men's dress.

Many top London makers travel widely in their business and have schedules for visiting places such as continental Europe, the Americas and parts of the British Commonwealth. Accordingly, you do not necessarily have to be in London to receive the full service with fittings of bespoke clothes. Moreover, after you have satisfactorily established patterns for shirts and lasts for bespoke shoes, fittings for these garments are not usual and changes would need to be made only as weight and bones change in time. **W.S. Foster & Son** and **Henry Maxwell** have in their collection of shoe lasts those of famous film director and producer Cecil B. de Mille and these seem to have incorporated possible alterations.

I have eschewed the vulgar excesses of monogrammed (or even *coroneted*) shirts and silken underwear, pyjamas and dressing gowns; although suits of silk pyjamas (for those who, unlike Winston Churchill and James Bond, have any use for pyjamas at all) are essentials for journeys on sleeper trains (for so long as 'sleepers' remain with us).

Visible designer labels are quite repulsive. Savile Row (type) clothes traditionally do not normally bear the maker's mark or label except inside the inside breast pocket, along with the date, its number and name of customer. I say 'Savile Row type' because fewer and fewer top tailors are exactly in 'the Row' and they come and go between there and the neighbouring streets: indeed, Brummell (as mentioned, with whom the worldwide reputation of London-made clothes began) patronized, according to his first biographer, Captain Jesse, tailors Schweitzer & Davidson, in Cork Street and Weston in Bond Street. He also patronized Meyer in Conduit Street (now **Meyer & Mortimer** in Sackville Street): either Meyer or Brummell invented the pantaloon trousers which Brummell was certainly the first to wear in fashionable circles – the drivers of the tumbrels and the husbands of *les tricoteuses* (the old women who sat around the guillotine watching and knitting, and roaring out their disgusting approval, as the heads rolled) wore a type of loose trousers – rather than breeches – hence their name '*sans culottes*' (literally 'without breeches').

Unfortunately, nearly all Brummell's records, including patterns and orders in the shop were lost as a result of enemy action in the Second World War, when Meyer & Mortimer (as they had become) also lost their Paris shop.

Ede & Ravenscroft, the country's oldest tailors (although they now also have premises in Burlington Gardens) are principally based in Chancery Lane. How wide the magic quadrangle expands *virtually* should depend upon an objective assessment of the goods themselves and value for money.

Bespoke shirts are, sometimes, discreetly monogrammed and very little else is. However, Lady Diana Cooper ordered a pair of monogrammed slippers for Winston Churchill. They had the initials facing outwards as though to dispel doubt as to the wearer's identity. (See A.L. Rowse, *Memories and Glimpses*, 1986.)

If you are going the whole hog to bespeak everything, be prepared for the fact that bespoke shoes may cost as much as, or even more than, a bespoke suit (as, indeed, they have for a long time) but they are likely, with proper care, to last longer and to mature and even to improve with age and wear. Obviously, the cost differentials between, say, bespoke shoes and suits can vary widely, depending on the materials employed in each: crocodile and vicuña, respectively, will increase the cost of the particular item considerably. Always remember that nothing should look too new. One should really hang and weather one's new tweeds, before wearing, much as one hangs game, before eating.

SOME EXAMPLES – OLD AND NEW – OF THE STYLE-CONSCIOUS

Some people go for a kind of uniform: Winston Churchill's **Turnbull & Asser** spotted bow ties (imitated by James Bond's inventor, Ian Fleming – who, according to Andrew Lycett, boasted of the 'Churchillian looseness' of his knot – and by Jeremy Paxman's predecessor, Robin Day – who did not, but claimed, instead, that he was following his father whose hero had been sometime Liberal Prime Minister Lord Rosebery); actor Yul Brynner's black everything; press baron Lord Northcliffe's **Henry Poole** blue suits and red spotted ties; television presenter Jeremy Clarkson and his jeans, blouson, practical boots and robust opinions; and Jonathan Ross in his baggy suits wielding his own interviewing shock tactics.

At the other extreme, there are the real mavericks: F.E. Smith (Winston Churchill's greatest friend, sometime Lord Chancellor, said

Ian Fleming, wreathed in smoke, and in a loosely knotted bow tie: photograph by Horst Tappe/Getty Images.

to have been the ablest man in the kingdom) turned up, in the early part of the Twentieth Century, at an official meeting with the Irish Republican leader, Michael Collins, without a silk hat and was berated by King George V for it and he also arrived at the Savoy in a brown lounge suit, demanding (and, by force of character, being served) dinner. However, there is nothing especially clever about being a maverick when everybody is at it.

Now is not just the age of the maverick, it is the age of the ignoramus maverick. F.E. Smith knew better and those who served him his dinner at the Savoy knew that he knew better; even George V knew that he knew better; on a visit to Sandringham, after the 'battle of the silk hat' (furiously waged in writing between the King's Private Secretary and 'F.E.' himself) George V showed 'F.E.' to the room in which he would sleep, lent him a terrier for company and then, despite the fact that there were footmen at hand on every side, the King and Emperor knelt, struck a match and lit the fire for him. (See the biography by F.E.'s son.)

I am going to advise according to ample means, moderately expended and not according to the superficially attractive policy of 'extravagance without bounds' which has been the cause of many a fallen house, even though, as Charles Baudelaire put it:

> the dandy does not wish to have money for its own sake; he would be content to be allowed to live indefinitely on credit; he leaves the coarse desire for money to baser mortals.

Before I launch into the fine detail, there are a few very general rules which, although now ignored by many (sometimes out of convenience and sometimes out of sheer ignorance), one should bear in mind.

- Strictly one should still always wear a dark suit in town (and never tweeds of any colour; except when coming, going or merely passing through) and black leather shoes (never brown or suede).
- Day ties may be any colour but, in the evening, when not in evening dress, dark suits and dark ties should be worn.
- Dark hats are worn in town and never straw, palm or tweed – and certainly not caps.

(When I refer to 'town', I mean the Metropolis; not, say, Truro, Cardiff, Cambridge or Bognor Regis.) These are old rules but there is no reason to suppose that, just because they are frequently broken (even by those who *do* know better), they no longer apply.

Moreover, so far as compliance with rules is concerned, just look at the prescriptions in the Decalogue itself!

There are also a few distinctions which need to be taken on board.

- 'Bespoke' garments (including shoes) are made from scratch to the customer's precise dimensions and according to his exact choice of materials and colours and style.
- 'Made to measure' garments are made to standard patterns and sizes and then adjusted to the customer's dimensions.
- 'Ready-made' or 'off the peg' garments are made in standard sizes and patterns and the customer takes potluck on pattern and fit.

I do not give a full exposition of historical aspects of dress such as dress at court (although I do touch on that subject under 'Very Formal Morning Dress'); I do not deal comprehensively with academic, legal, naval or military dress, or with local dress variations such as kilts and I do not deal with the protocol of wearing decorations to certain functions. A general starting place for such information is John Morgan's *Debrett's New Guide to Etiquette and Modern Manners*.

Finally, as general background, always bear in mind a passage in Lord Chesterfield's letters; to the effect that: 'A man of sense carefully avoids any particular character in his dress; he is accurately clean for his own sake; but all the rest is for other people's.'

They say that any good story has a beginning, a middle and an end. I shall start with the undergarments and general haberdashery but I do not promise to proceed in any strictly logical fashion afterwards.

Chapter One

General Haberdashery

No perfumes – but very fine linen and plenty of it – and country washing.

THIS WAS a dictum of Beau Brummell, recounted in Captain Jesse's Life of Beau Brummell. But, by these words, he did not mean: 'don't use cologne at all' – because he did (from **J. Floris**) – he meant that linens should not be scented, in storage, with lavender or anything of the kind.

INTRODUCTORY

There are few pleasures so innocently satisfying as a dip in the tropical ocean, followed by a hot and a cold shower, a brisk rub down and then dressing in fresh, crisp linen. When it is of the first quality, the satisfaction is doubled. The Edwardians would have changed three or more times a day; for the morning until after luncheon; for the afternoon's activities and then, after six o'clock, into evening dress. Of course, very few people do this anymore. But there are days in many lives when the occasions call for this performance. Seize these opportunities.

There is no substitute for bespoke shirts and there are some made in the gods' quad which are the best shirts in the world. Principally, I would recommend **Budd** (especially for evening and formal morning shirts), **New & Lingwood**, **Turnbull & Asser** and **Hilditch & Key**. These shops also sell everything that you will need in the haberdashery line. If you bespeak shirts, remember that you can have exactly what you want; for example, if you wear a wrist watch, you can have the cuff on that side made slightly wider. You are not stuck with shirts that undo all the way down; you can have tunic-cut shirts that you pull on over your head because the bottom half of the front is solid material. Moreover, a bespoke shirt will fit like a second skin – up to 28 body measurements are taken to make the pattern. Equally, you can have them made easy fitting, if you prefer.

SOCKS AND STOCKINGS

Of course, the 'chuddies' go on first – and I favour boxer shorts because they seem far less ridiculous and more comfortable than any of the other types which squash one up, but they are, physiologically, in the middle part and no good story starts in the middle. Have, say, three dozen pairs of wool and nylon (cashmere or cashmere and merino mix, if you are really going for it) *half hose* (i.e. up to the knee). Plain cotton versions are available for the summer. With two very specific exceptions, socks should match trousers. The first exception is red socks which, for some reason that I cannot exactly explain, always raise a smile, especially when worn with a dark suit. Maybe it is something to do with a glimpse of the daring and dashing and dangerous lurking beneath the trousers, suggesting that these qualities may lurk in the wearer too. The second exception is shooting stockings which are normally bright.

Emma Willis'
shooting stockings.

Except on the tennis court, eschew calf and ankle socks and so avoid the stigma properly and universally attached to *mezza calza* (often menacingly evidenced by an expanse of flesh between trouser ends and sock tops on TV interviews and chat shows). Indeed avoid *anything* at half-mast. *Mezza calza* is Italian for 'half sock' and to call someone this in Italy means basically that they are a peasant.

Have also, say, six pairs of silk half hose evening stockings and the same quantity of woollen shooting stockings. Budd is good for socks and best for evening stockings. They were established in 1910, originally at number 4 Piccadilly Arcade and they are the only remaining original occupants of this Edwardian Arcade. They make, on the premises, in a family-owned firm, some of the best shirts in the world and, arguably, the very best evening shirts. They do not have a website, an email address or even a brochure. When I asked about this, their Mr Rowley politely but firmly explained 'We're shirt-makers'. Like **Bristol Cars**, they have no dealerships or franchises. If you want a Budd shirt, you attend their shop, just as always. This is a quite delightful and resolute exception in the modern world.

There is also New & Lingwood. In 1865, Miss New and Mr Lingwood (who would later marry each other) set up shop in Eton and they have close links, as suppliers, with the school. In 1922 they opened additional Jermyn Street premises but after being bombed out in the Second World War they moved to their present site at the Jermyn Street end of the Piccadilly Arcade. In 1972, the old shoe-making firm of Poulsen Skone joined them. More recently, the shirt-makers Bowring Arundel also joined the firm.

Cording's are good for strong, woollen shooting stockings and garters. **Emma Willis** in Jermyn Street runs up a superb merino and cashmere version in a variety of colours.

Smalls, chuddies or boxer shorts

'Chuddies' was originally a slang Punjabi word for underpants. It received recognition in the *Oxford English Dictionary* as a word in English usage as a result of the satirical television programme *Goodness Gracious Me*.

Have, say, two dozen pairs of coloured linen or cotton, balloon-seated to avoid the phenomenon known to modern children as the 'wedgie' and, especially if made of linen which tends not to cling, tight enough around the thigh to avoid unintentional 'flashing' at the tailor's fittings of the outer garments. If you're frivolously going bespoke on these (maybe at Budd), a mother of pearl or 'shell' fly button could be added, for additional security). To be labelled as 'Irish' linen, goods must be knitted or woven in Ireland; however, the flax from which the material is made now comes from northern Europe.

Lewins do well cut ready-made boxers (not balloon-seated) but, if you want tradition and easy-fitting, ready-made comfort for your money, go down the Piccadilly Arcade to New & Lingwood. Hilditch & Key do a good range of silk 'longjohns' for wear beneath tweeds – the scratchy trousers and knickerbockers of which are *never*, in the UK and Eire, lined. This firm was founded by shirt-makers Charles F. Hilditch and W. Graham Key in 1899, originally in the Tottenham Court Road.

DAY SHIRTS

Have, say, two or three dozen day shirts for town (bearing in mind: never wear strongly patterned shirts with strongly patterned suits; also avoid, if one is being especially pure, spotted ties with striped shirts – or even striped ties

Mother of pearl is carved from the nacreous inside of the shells of molluscs such as oysters and mussels. It is also used, plain or carved, to ornament handles of such things as daggers and revolvers: the best caviar spoons are made from mother of pearl – because it does not tarnish the taste, unlike metal.

with spotted shirts). The sensible part of this was advice given to me by Mr Matthews of **Davies & Son**. I tend to go for plain white, cream and pale blue, in a variety of weaves and materials.

There are different collar shapes and sizes, including: cutaway collars and pointed collars; there are double cuffs, single cuffs, barrelled cuffs and surgeon's cuffs and all double cuffs can be mitred, rounded or squared off. Single cuffs tend to be usual on country and weekend shirts. The barrelled cuffs, by Turnbull & Asser, were made famous by Sean Connery as James Bond. These are double cuffs, which are buttoned and called by their makers 'cocktail cuffs'.

The materials available for shirts are numerous and include: West Indian sea island cotton, Italian batiste (lightweight cottons) poplin (also known as tabinet, it was originally a silk warp and cotton weft worsted yarn, deriving its usual name from where it was first made in Papeline, Avignon – now it is a fine cotton fabric), Oxford (a basket weave cotton), Royal Oxford, broadcloth silk, Swiss cotton, Egyptian mako (which tends to shrink by up to 2.5 per cent in the first few washes), Viyella (originally this was a merino wool and cotton blend, now it is also a brand name), Irish linen, cashmere and vicuña. Some of these materials come in a variety of weaves, such as ribbed twill and herringbone. Be aware that the looser weaves, and especially herringbones, will rub and wear around the collar and cuffs quite quickly.

Sean Connery was taken under the wing of film director Terence Young, who coached him for the role of James Bond; even to the extent of introducing Connery to his tailors and his shirt-maker, Turnbull & Asser, who had just designed this cuff and thus it was chosen as a signature garment for Bond. Terence Young directed *Dr No*, *From Russia With Love* and *Thunderball* and is acknowledged as the inspiration for the screen persona and appearance of the

James Bond of these early films – less sinister (and much more humorous) than the character as portrayed in the books. Sean Connery is, certainly by a vast majority of those over 40, regarded as the definitive screen James Bond.

Hawes & Curtis were founded in 1913 and claim the invention of the Windsor tie knot – I have not included diagrams of such things, as it is better to ask a haberdasher to demonstrate them for you. They used to tailor for nearly forgotten 1930s international star of stage and screen Jack Buchanan, standing next to whom Bing Crosby said made him feel like a cab driver. They also tailored for British actor Robert Donat who won the Oscar for best actor in his

Inset: A cutaway collar style available in New & Lingwood's bespoke range.

Turnbull & Asser barrelled or cocktail shirt cuff.

role as 'Mr Chips' in the black and white classic *Good-bye Mr Chips* – in the same year that *Gone With the Wind* was released. Now the haberdashery side of Hawes & Curtis, who used to do for King Edward VIII (who abdicated to devote the rest of his life to frivolity) and Noel Coward, make ready-made shirts and sell them at very reasonable (not to say, low) prices. They even do shaped, waisted models.

If you do bespeak your shirts, make sure that if, for example, your tailor has noted and allowed for a drop on a shoulder (i.e. in common with many people, you may have one shoulder lower than the other – called a 'drop'), you pass this information on to your shirt-maker; otherwise, unless your shirt-maker makes exactly the same allowance as the tailor, you might end up with one shirt sleeve hanging lower from your coat cuff than the other. This *once* happened to me and it is, I assure you, most annoying.

Buttons on bespoke shirts often used to have three holes (rather than four) and were sewn on by hand; of course this is no longer the case. Still, bespoke shirts should have proper mother of pearl or 'shell' buttons. Some better ready-made shirts also have these.

On the subject of showing cuff: if your shirts and suits are bespoke, the question should not arise. However, if you need to consider the issue just remember that the only real sin is to show *too much* shirt cuff because this plainly demonstrates that something does not fit correctly. The usual modern rule seems to be for about half an inch of shirt cuff to show. However, some really fine English tailors cut coat sleeves long and there simply is no room for any shirt cuff to show through. In *Parkinson's Law* the author C. Northcote Parkinson, as well as noting that, as the British Empire declined in size, the number of officials in the Colonial Office *increased*, observed that Americans show cuff and the British don't. Over-preoccupation with this issue would, however, be tiresome.

BRACES

Tailors and the vendors of them (all over the place) and Americans call them 'suspenders'. *We* call them 'braces' because 'suspenders' tends to call up quite different images. There is really only one type: Thurston's red box cloth with white suede button suspenders (beware of brown button suspenders because the colour rubs off on the clothing) on waxed cord – or white silk and white suede for evening. I know that red box cloth has, in this connection, had a bad press thanks to the 'Yuppie' culture of the 1980s. However, there is no need to be intimidated by this. A couple of pairs of braces at a time will do as they almost last for ever (eventually, the metal tends to tarnish and then the box cloth balds and frays but I have never known them actually to break or rip). I dare say that if one were buried in them they might actually decay after a century or so in the ground but no problem is likely to arise until the Day of Judgement. They are in the same category as the suits which I had made by **Davies & Son**, superbly constructed with the humorous guarantee: 'Our suits may not fit, sir, but they last forever'. (Weight gains have now put some of these to the back of the wardrobe. A similar phrase is: 'it fits where it touches'.)

TIES

Although some maintain that the sales figures for ties say otherwise, ties seem to be in desuetude because several modern 'celebrities' will not wear them and where such people lead many follow. Moreover, Notting Hill Tories think that the *petit-bourgeois* majority of active British voters are likely to warm to Old Etonian politicians who wear suits with open-necked shirts. Whether *they* will ever lead (again) remains to be seen. I suspect that many of these people see open-necked shirts as making a Byronic statement of modernity, if not of rebellious potential. Little do they realize that at least one of the famous pictures of Byron with an open-necked shirt was originally a portrait of him as he actually appeared – in a cravat. It is utterly inconceivable that he (or anyone else) would have wandered around town – let alone into, say, Watier's Club – with an open-necked shirt. The cravat in the portrait was later painted out – why, I don't know. However, to my mind, it would take much more than the examples of modern Britons to wipe out a tradition which began with neck cloths, centuries ago.

There is some evidence that the ancient Chinese and even the Romans, on occasion, wore cloths around their necks. The modern tie probably has its clearest origin in the wearing of neck cloths by Croatian soldiers in Paris in 1635. This fashion was copied by the French who called wearing the garment going 'à la Croate' – later this garment became known as a 'cravat'. This fashion was introduced in England at the time of the restoration of King Charles II in 1660 and the cravat and stock gradually replaced the lace *jabot*, which had previously been worn (and is worn again with Henry Poole's shrieval court dress).

The wearing of ties should be encouraged not least because the tie is the one item in which an individual may give vent to his own particular ideas without becoming the subject of too much scorn. It is also a most respectable garment – which may account for its demise: it is not Jack-The-Lad enough. Here the world is your oyster and many suppliers make exclusive hand-made ties: famously **Hermes** (founded by Thierry Hermes in 1837, originally specializing in leather goods and saddlery; the famous scarf first appeared in the early 1930s) or **Charvet** (a French shirt and tie maker).

You will need a woven silver silk tie for

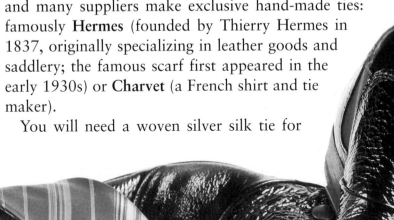

formal morning wear, a woven black tie for funerals, a few ribbed or woven black silk bow ties for the evening and some white Marcella formal evening ties (to match shirt and waistcoat) for full fig – which is often called 'white tie'. There is no reason why one should not commission ties on a bespoke basis; just be aware that it takes a yard of expensive cloth to make a tie (because of the way it has to be cut: against the bias and normally in three pieces) before you add the labour.

At Oxford it is said that club/school/college/regimental/association ties, as we know them, derive from an occasion in 1880 when men at Exeter College Oxford tied their striped hatbands around their necks as a sign of collegiate unity. It is suggested that it is otiose to wear such a tie to a gathering of the club or an alumni association event, because everyone there is a member. Such ties should, therefore, be reserved for other occasions. Some say that these ties are, with a few notable exceptions, always 'naff'. The exceptions are: the Garrick Club tie (which I have heard very nicely described as 'salmon and cucumber'), the Old Etonian tie and the garish Marylebone Cricket Club (MCC) tie (striped orange and mustard yellow a colour combination sometimes referred to as 'becon and eggs'). **Benson & Clegg** supply many association ties, although not the MCC or Garrick ties which are available through the clubs themselves.

If you are like Roald Dahl's Uncle Oswald, of course, you will damn the expense and have your own spider silk gathered, spun, dyed and woven first, but remember that A. Sulka of Bond Street are no longer there to superintend the whole process for you (or, indeed, to make your pyjamas, dressing gowns and smoking jackets). After a good deal of research, I have discovered that they are not even still in New York, Paris or Chicago but their London workers (or some of them) were taken over by **Alfred Dunhill** (whose famous logo is a discreet white spot; originally in the Euston Road, they progressed to motoring accessories, known as Dunhill's 'Motorities'). Sometimes, Sulka items can be found second-hand. However, we may well reflect how are the mighty fallen when we learn that relevant **Harrods'** buyers, in 2006, had not even heard of the firm which figged out Noel Coward in those most famous dressing gowns – symbolic garments of the art deco era.

Amos Sulka set up shop in Lower Broadway in 1895 and Sulka labels on their supremely luxurious merchandise proclaimed: 'New York London Paris' (some also include 'Chicago', 'San Francisco' and 'Palm Beach'), for a century, until the brand was wholly closed down by its new owners in or around 2002. Why did they buy the business if they didn't want the name? Presumably, just to rub out the competition. I distinctly recall walking, at about this time, to their distinguished, marble-fronted Bond Street premises and, being unable to find the shop where it should be, I walked up and down, in angry confusion, for some time, until I had to confront the bitter truth: that the old apophthegm, *tout lasse, tout casse, tout passe* has to apply even to such an icon as Sulka; favoured as it had been by

---

Spider silk (gossamer) is one of the wonders of nature; the dragline (which spiders hang on) of ordinary garden spider silk is 0.003mm in diameter, compared with 0.03 for each strand of silkworm silk (the silk of the larvae of *Bombyx mori*) and yet the silk of a spider in the genus *Nephila* – the golden orb weaving spider – (at 0.008mm) is twice as strong as silkworm silk. It is probably less strong than the best steel (iron and carbon) like for like in terms of diameter but this spider silk is far stronger than steel like for like in terms of weight. Moreover, spider silk is, undoubtedly, the strongest natural fibre and can be produced by up to 7 glands on some spiders. The silk of the golden orb spider is the most sought-after for textiles. As may be readily imagined, it doesn't come cheap. A good starting point on this general subject is Paul Hillyard's *The Book of the Spider* (1994).

such as Rudolph Valentino, F. Scott Fitzgerald, Gary Cooper, Clarke Gable, the Kennedys, the Rockefellers and Winston Churchill, as well as Noel Coward: *in manus tuas Domine*.

Fortunately, New & Lingwood and also Budd have a tremendous selection of ties; including Ancient Madder ties (foulard silk traditionally dyed with natural vegetable dyes from *Rubia tinctorum*, largely in muted reds, blues, greens and ochre). Once again, Emma Willis is also strongly contending in relation to hand-made ties.

Finally, on ties, the standard day Four in Hand tie should be tied so that it possesses a vertical dimple in the middle, below the knot. It gets the name 'Four in Hand' from the Four in Hand Carriage Club (i.e. a club for those who drove in carriages pulled by four horses) whose membership favoured this knot. The lower end of this dimple is the ideal nestling place to put a pin. The 'Windsor' knot is, traditionally, seen as a mark of a bounder; interestingly, the late Duke of Windsor, after whom it is named, did not use it: his ties were puffed up because they were lined with heavy material.

HANDKERCHIEFS – BRIEF HISTORY, NOTE AND GENERAL WARNING

The use of handkerchiefs in England dates from at least the reign of Richard II (reigned 1377–99): his Household Rolls include expenditure on them. Moreover, handkerchiefs would have been well enough known to the groundlings in 1603, the date of Shakespeare's tragedy *Othello*. Purloining and planting Desdemona's distinctive handkerchief (a gift from Othello) in Cassio's room was the central plank upon which the evil Iago based his ploy to beguile Othello into the mistaken belief that Desdemona had betrayed him with Cassio.

So far as current use of handkerchiefs is concerned: in town, purists do *not* sport a handkerchief (whether coloured or not) in the breast pocket, despite the examples set by, amongst others: Winston Churchill, the Duke of Edinburgh and the present Prince of Wales, Cary Grant, Noel Coward and Jack Buchanan. One chap I know insists on defying me on this and *his* reason is that the first woman MP, Nancy Lady Astor, approved of hankies in breast pockets. He completely overlooks the rather glaring fact that Lady Astor was a woman. But there we are. I suspect that the real reason is that he had already made a heavy investment in decorative handkerchiefs before I corrected him. On this, in my view, those who sport a hankie in town (and their advisers) are wrong. *Debrett's* seems to support me in this, in that they put hankies in the same category as pens.

A snuff handkerchief may be carried in the sleeve, coat pocket or stuffed in the waistcoat or hat wherever one may be; except in the evening when it should be white silk. With a *country* suit, a coloured handkerchief *may* adorn the breast pocket. Never ever sport a matching tie and handkerchief unless you manage an out-of-town superstore. Clashing ties and handkerchiefs are more inner suburban bank manager or clueless upwardly mobile. Handkerchiefs must always be shaken out before use and *never* carried folded up.

White lawn handkerchiefs are made of plain weave linen – the name 'lawn' deriving from Laon in France where it used to be made – and they are fairly standard for offering (virgin) to damsels in

Attar of Roses is an essential oil, obtained by steam distillation of the petals of *Rosa damascena mill.* (damask rose), largely grown in Bulgaria, Turkey, Russia, India, China and Iran; it takes many pounds of petals to make one tiny phial of this oil. It was a rose of this type which was planted at the head of the grave of Edward FitzGerald, in Boulge Churchyard, Suffolk, in 1893, by the Omar Khayya'm Society. In 1884, an artist from the *Illustrated London News*, called William Simpson, brought back a rose hip from the grave of Omar Khayya'm in Na'ishapu'r, in Persia. This was sent by Bernard Quaritch (the original publisher, in 1859, of the 1st edn of Edward FitzGerald's famous paraphrase translation of the *Ruba'iya't* of Omar Khayya'm), to the Royal Horticultural Society at Kew where the bush was propagated. In 1972, the Government of Iran supplemented this planting with more at the foot of the grave.

distress. The excellent **Irish Linen Company** formerly in the Burlington Arcade supplies them.

Have white and coloured silk handkerchiefs made abroad and stitched all around by hand for about 50 pence each – or pay almost a hundred times as much in the quad. They are excellent for the evening or, if, like Soames Forsyte (of *The Forsyte Saga*), you have a sensitive nose when suffering from a head cold.

Snuff handkerchiefs are ubiquitous and plentiful in Jermyn Street: brightly coloured cotton to disguise the use of snuff. I once knew someone who always had a very clean one and a very used one on his person: they were denoted, respectively, the 'commissioned officer' and the 'other ranks'. He used a dark strong snuff called Fribourg & Treyer's Macouba (scented with attar of roses), which was favoured by Brummell and (along with many other good things) is still available from **G. Smith & Sons** cigar shop.

SCARF/MUFFLER

Paisley-patterned silk-backed cashmere is usual. Beware of novelty items, football colours or even your old college colours beyond the age of 30 (since, by then, parading the fact that you got through university looks like the height of your achievement – even if it really is). Ede & Ravenscroft and New & Lingwood normally have very good selections. You should also have a white silk evening scarf and Budd stock very good examples in white, cream or black. The **Yves St Laurent** evening scarf is also a work of art.

GLOVES

Gloves and gauntlets (extended gloves with a forearm covering) were known in England, from at least the time of the Norman Conquest, in 1066. They were badges of honour and distinction and throwing down the gauntlet to one's adversary was the signal for a challenge to a duel. French master glover Xavier Jouvin (1800–44) invented the system for standard patterns, which meant that gloves were produced in standard sizes. From the Seventeenth Century, London has been the world centre of first-class glove production.

Spy

Hemrose Dalziel Ltd., Watford & London.

"To the manner born."

(Mr. Reginald Corbet).

Dunhill driving gloves: the ultimate.

All gloves, except Alfred Dunhill's superlative driving gloves and Budd's evening gloves, come from **Pickett** in the Burlington Arcade (now that ancient Lord's, also once in that Arcade, has gone) or from **Chester Jefferies**. It is possible, besides buying off the shelf, to have gloves bespoke or made to order in standard sizes. Bespoke gloves cost very little more than ready-made gloves. There is no need to go as far as suggested by an apocryphal story that Brummell used to have different makers for the main part, *on the one hand*, and thumbs, on the other, of his gloves.

Alfred Dunhill driving gloves

The illustration speaks volumes: they are instant classics. These gloves would be equally at home on the wheel of a 1960 Zagato-bodied 406 **Bristol** motorcar – or their latest Bristol Fighter – or even the Bristol Blenheim Speedster (the last car mentioned is available to order only).

Grey mocha gloves

These are made of softest shorn sheepskin. Have a couple of pairs of these. They should have quite prominent hand stitching and are ideal for everyday city wear.

A range of Pickett gloves; including calf and, second from the right, peccary and a driving glove.

Peccary gloves

According to a sometime manager of Lord's, these should bear some scar tissue to demonstrate that the beast which ultimately lay down its life in such a noble cause was indeed a wild peccary *Tayassu pecari* (a boar-like creature) in South America and had been in a tusk fight or two. These, or deerskin gloves, would do very well as hunting gloves.

Black leather gloves

Have a pair of these – for funerals only.

> The Burlington Arcade, opened in 1819, is one of the world's first shopping malls. It connects Burlington Gardens with Piccadilly. The Royal Opera Arcade, on the site of Market Lane, linking Charles II Street with Pall Mall, dates from 1818. The Burlington Arcade was built in the garden of Burlington House (now home to the Royal Academy), to the order of Lord George Cavendish and it is still policed by Beadles in toppers who enforce rules against open umbrellas and running: 'Excuse me, sir, would you kindly refrain from doing that; *this is the Burlington Arcade*, you know'. It is certainly one of the world's best shopping malls. The others in the 'quad' are the later Piccadilly Arcade and Princes Arcade – both connecting Piccadilly and Jermyn Street. Unfortunately, most recent examples of malls elsewhere in England do not live up to these prototypes or sell goods of anything like the same quality. Maybe the Arcade inspired William Hargreaves to write the music hall song 'Burlington Bertie', performed by his wife Ella Shields at the Birkenhead Argyle Theatre in October 1914 and recorded by her in 1915. It was most famously sung by the spirited Vesta Tilley in a bashed-up topper all skew-whiff and with the 'Hyde Park drawl', briefly to cheer the generation which lost so many.

Chapter Two

General Day Wear: Suits and Coats

A man should look as though he has chosen his clothes with intelligence, put them on with care . . . and then forgotten all about them. (Sir (Edwin) Hardy Amies)

LOUNGE SUITS – INTRODUCTION

THESE are very necessary items for town and country. One should have these in as large a quantity as reasonably practicable – perhaps, according to ample means moderately applied, six for town and six for the country on the go at the outset and one or two each a year on top.

First-rate Savile Row bespoke suits in very reasonable but not rare cloths are now around the £3,000 mark (including VAT). However, outside the Row and the gods' quad, you can get a very passable bespoke suit for around £1,000. Part of the difference in price is, of course, a reflection of the difference in overheads. However, far away from the Row you will be taking potluck on cut and general quality. Good ready-made suits are going to be in the region of £500–£600 and are best bought for even less in the sales – for the last

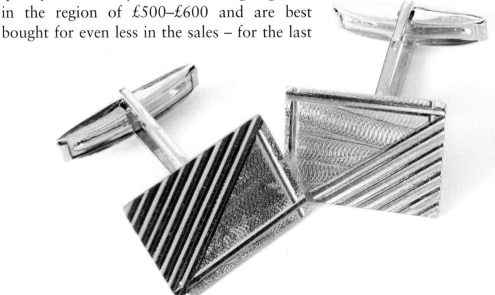

couple of years New & Lingwood lightweight suits have been reduced from £550 to £295.

THE RAW MATERIALS

Overall, you will probably find that a variety in cloth weights will be more useful than a variety of colours and patterns. For English

Vicuña comes from a Peruvian member of the camel family. They are small *wild* creatures and the fleece is harvested every other year, when the creatures are herded into enclosures and shorn in a system which has changed little since the time of the Incas; except that shorn animals are no longer slaughtered afterwards – not least because of their comparative rarity. Each creature renders only about 250g of the luxurious, downy undercoat and you would need the harvest from 40 animals to render enough for just one topcoat. It is reassuringly expensive and you are looking, at current rates, at about £5,000 just for the cloth for one suit. Larger-than-life Lord Castlerosse (later 6th Earl of Kenmare) used to wear evening clothes made of inky blue vicuña and exclaim: 'What's the good of being a viscount, if you can't live on credit?'

The Incas believed that only their royal family should wear vicuña. The singular merits of this cloth derive from the fineness of each vicuña hair which is between 10 and 12 microns. This is to be compared with ordinary domestic sheep (*Ovis aries*) at 30 microns or human hair at about 50 microns. Next comes angora (*Capra aegarus hircus* – the common name is from the Turkish *Ankara kecisi*) which is from a goat (mohair): this comes in at about 11–15 microns; merino sheep's wool is 12–22; guanaco (*Lama guanicoe*, a large South American llama) is 14–18; royal baby alpaca (*Vicugna pacos*) is at 19; cashmere (*capra hircus blythi*) is at 14–19 and alpaca is at 18–40. There are mixes of these wools – especially with silk and linen, for lighter fabrics.

summer wear and tropical places, you will need cloth in the lighter weights. The best sort of normal cloth is woollen worsted (normally of merino wool) and it comes in grades known as super 100s to 220 - 120, 150s and so on (this figure relates to the fineness of the yarn) and super lightweight worsted or mohair. Then there is also raw silk (which comes as dupioni or tussore).

However, if you really want to go for it, there is an enormous range of weights, weaves and patterns. **Holland & Sherry** is one of the best known cloth houses around and can supply virtually anything on the market. But if you want the rarest and best cloth of all, vicuña, you (or your tailor) will need to go to a merchant called **Loro Piana** in Bond Street. The suiting in this is 93 per cent vicuña and 7 per cent silk mix – the silk is to keep the shape.

WOVEN CLOTHS

There is a bewildering array of cloth weaves, patterns and types and it is not the purpose of this book to recommend any in particular because choice in such detail is a purely personal matter. However, some general outline may be helpful.

As mentioned above, there are super worsteds at between 100 and 220mm long, which weigh in at between 7–9 ounces. Some good examples of the lighter fabrics are the Holland & Sherry Whisperlight and Capri ranges or the **Dormeuil** Microtwist range.

For autumn and winter weight lounge suits there are worsteds and flannels (flannel is a loosely woven woollen yarn, originally made in Wales in the Seventeenth Century), typically at between 10–13 ounces (and note that, here, imperial measurement still seems to prevail). Modern living conditions mean that there is little demand for lounge suit fabrics at 16 ounces or more. However, you should definitely have at least one suit in West of England Tweed, which will be quite heavy. Other famous cloth brands are **Scabal** and **Wain Shiell**.

Every good wardrobe has an archive which should be cleared out periodically but only when items are fit to go to the bonfire or local municipal dump, after exhaustive garden wear.

DETAIL OF THE SUITS

The town suit

I should advise having probably two or three piece suits in double-breasted style for the town. It is mainly personal preference but I feel that the double-breasted style is more metropolitan – the front echoing formal frock coats. The detail on these could very reasonably be as follows. The coat should have three gently sloping main, side coat pockets (normally with flaps), including a ticket pocket on the right-hand side. You could have six buttons on the front of the coat, including the two 'display' buttons (one on either side at the top). You could match up Brandenburg cuffs (turned-back cuffs) on the coat sleeves with cuffs (turn-ups to most of us) on the trousers. It is a myth that one should not have trouser turn-ups on a double-breasted lounge suit. If you do have the double-breasted style, it does not matter that much whether you have a waistcoat as well, because the front is well covered. It would be best to have a single-breasted waistcoat with a double-breasted coat. Equally, it would be perfectly in order to have either a single-breasted or double-breasted waistcoat (if a double-breasted waistcoat, have lapels too) with a single-breasted coat.

Suits normally have coats. 'Jacket' includes the following: a dinner jacket, a shooting jacket, a smoking jacket, a Norfolk jacket, a hacking jacket, a mess jacket (otherwise known as a monkey jacket or a bum-freezer) or a reefer jacket.

Silk coat linings can be as your whimsy takes you (maybe bright but probably unpatterned). In any event, you will find that each firm has its own house-style for sleeve linings and inner trouser trimmings – and they normally come in a variety of stripes on white or cream. These linings just appear and there is little point in trying to kick over the traces and ask for something else. On the subject of kicking over the traces: a few times, I asked for single-breasted suit coats with square fronts – not rounded off. The first time, this request was met with a sucking of teeth and a sideways look and the question whether I was 'sure'. Sure, I was sure. Anyway, the coat was cut quite square, except for, 'just blunted-off, sir' – then an expression of quiet amazement that it *did* work. Well, the blunting off got progressively more aggressive until I gave up. A similar thing happened with an inky blue mohair suit which I bespoke once: there was never any discussion of lining material and it was finished in black lining, including the sleeves – as though to tell me: 'if you will wear a *mohair* suit, and in *town*, sir, we have to be conservative with the lining, don't we? My guv'nor always lined mohair in black and his guv'nor before *him*. If it was good enough for *them*, sir, then it's quite good enough for *us*.' Most of the time, they have a point – and it is far easier to go with the flow.

The modern convention for vents is that a single-breasted coat has none, one or two vents and a double-breasted coat has none or two vents, as you wish.

On cuff buttons: a lot of tosh has been written (some of it in reputable national newspapers). The rule, quite simply, is that you may have as many or few as you like – as long as any lower middle class insecurities will not be shaken by remarks about 'lost a button off his cuff', if you dare to have three. Curiously, there is no similar remark about just having two – or even one. One is a little bit 'Carnaby Street' (a London street, central to the adventurous fashion designers of the 'Swinging [19]60s' and their 'Peacock Revolution'). However, four is usual and it is usual too (even if slightly regrettable) to have only the lower two made with real buttonholes and the top two as dummies. **Anderson & Sheppard** make them all dummies – unless you ask nicely.

Anderson & Sheppard were founded in 1906. Per Anderson was trained by the renowned Frederick Scholte. Anderson & Sheppard famously used not to give interviews but their management has changed and they have become open and approachable.

In their former premises (in Savile Row – they are now in Old Burlington Street), Fred Astaire used to roll up the rug and dance on the parquet floor to test the fit of his coats (strange how evocative that image remains). Rudolph Valentino was another regular customer.

Double-breasted coats have a jigger button inside the top front left-hand side to attach to the outer buttonhole on the right-hand side – to keep the parts together; one should not really do up the lower button on a double-breasted coat. Following the Edwardian custom, leave the end button on single-breasted *day* waistcoats

George Sanders in a double-breasted suit and waistcoat as Favell (Rebecca's favourite cousin), talking to Judith Anderson as Mrs Danvers (with Joan Fontaine as the second Mrs de Winter, Laurence Olivier as Maxim de Winter and C. Aubrey Smith as the Chief Constable) from the Hitchcock/Selznick film of Rebecca: *photograph by SNAP/Rex Features.*

undone. Some tailors even make them so that the last button cannot be done up at all because of the distance between button and buttonhole. This custom is supposed to derive from King Edward VII who got so rotund that he had to undo the last button and it became an imitative fashion, which endures to this day. However, do not leave any buttons undone on an *evening* waistcoat.

Behind the buttonhole on the coat lapel it is usual to have a small loop to hold the stem of your buttonhole flower. If you are given to buttonhole flowers it is as well specifically to ask for a larger lapel buttonhole.

Cloth patterns for city suits are many and varied. Staples are: chalk-stripe flannel; pinstripes, nailhead, plain or cable-stripe, hopsack, windowpane checks and birds-eye; even a Glen Urquhart check, in woollen worsteds – the latter made famous by the late Duke of Windsor, when he had been Prince of Wales (indeed, sometimes now it is called 'Prince of Wales check' – although it must be said that this pattern is more for travelling or for country life).

Buttons for coats and waistcoats are various: horn in different colours, mother of pearl (maybe with light weight suits), plastics and buttons covered in the cloth of the suit. Sometimes woven leather buttons are used on shooting jackets.

So far as trousers are concerned: there should be two pleats on each side of the trouser waistband and these should face inwards - that is to say that the inside of the fold should face the centre of the trousers.

Zips instead of fly buttons on trousers were the innovation of Lord Mountbatten of Burma and were described by the magazine *London Life* (7 April 1934) as something, which might 'become one of the most important developments of men's fashions since knee breeches'. This time-saving innovation was taken up by Simpson (Piccadilly) of blessed memory in their distinctive **Daks** brand, when they were in their superb, purpose-built shop still standing at 203–206 Piccadilly. That brand is also noted for the introduction, in 1934, of the self-supporting waistband ('Daks' tops'), comprising side buckles; discarding braces. 'Daks' derives from the words 'Dad's slacks' – although there is nothing remotely fuddy-duddy about these clothes. The brand is still sold from a shop on the Jermyn Street side of the great art deco store from where they traded from 1936.

A fob pocket on the inside right in the waistband of the trousers is extremely useful – for coins; once it would have held a watch.

The country suit

Much of the above detail would apply equally to country suits, subject to the following. I would suggest having single-breasted three-piece suits for the country with one, two or three buttons down the front. You are very likely to want to have at least some of these made in tweed.

You will also probably wish to have suit trousers with the alternative of plus twos or plus fours breeches on a couple of them. Plus twos have an overhang of two inches below the knee and plus fours have a four inch overhang. If you wish to see a vast selection of tweeds, try **W. Bill**, in Savile Row, or **Johnston's** of Elgin, Morayshire. If you want your tweeds made up north of the border, there is **Campbell's** of Beauly. Lovat tweed is a nice colour: the particular shade of green reputedly being a Lord Lovat's interpretation of the combined visual effects of bluebells and primroses, seen across Loch Morar. One should certainly have one set of tweeds in brown and white hound's-tooth with a Norfolk jacket and plus twos and a mid-grey flannel suit is always useful for travelling.

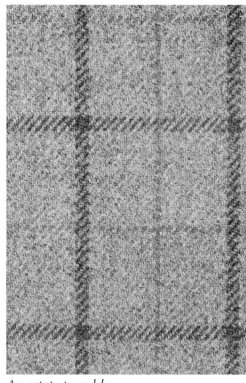

An estate tweed by Johnston's of Elgin.

'Tweed' derives from the old Scots word 'tweel' meaning 'twill'. There is an urban legend that a clerk at a cloth merchant's misspelled it and that is how the word 'tweed' came into use. It is said by tweed manufacturers Johnston's, established in 1797 in Elgin, that Lord Elcho's Hodden Grey tweed, dating from the mid-Nineteenth Century, is the origin of the colour khaki later taken up by the army as camouflage (see E. Harrison, *Scottish Estate Tweeds*, 1995). Hodden Grey tweed is a mix of white and ruddy brown. Of course, in the mid-Nineteenth Century, the soldiers used to charge around like moving targets, in bright red coats. The various estate tweeds were developed on the Highland estates to clothe the keepers and ghillies and comprise a kind of uniform, sometimes linked to the clan tartan or a colour in it. The main colours chosen for each derive from the colours of the landscape in which they will be worn to provide camouflage and so prevent the game being frightened off when people are shooting and stalking. Even though some of the colours used are bold and would show up a wearer in the street, they are surprisingly effective in the locality for which they are designed. The world-famous Harris Tweed from the Outer Hebrides is dyed with natural lichen dyes, which are responsible for the characteristic small specks of colour and the distinctive smell.

Tropical weight and touring suiting

For bespoke tropical weight suiting and touring clothes, one could do no better than **Norton & Sons** who now incorporate E. Tautz and J. Hoare. E. Tautz made such items for Winston Churchill in the early Twentieth Century and Norton & Sons made Colonel John Blashford-Snell's 'Explorer' suit when he made the first descent of the Blue Nile. They had also been a favoured tailor of Rittmeister Manfred Albrecht Freiherr von Richthofen (the 'Red Baron', a

German fighter ace in the First World War).

Norton & Sons was originally founded by Walter Grant Norton, in Strand, in 1821. They moved to Lombard Street where they gained a reputation as City tailors, before moving to Savile Row where they gained the Prussian King Wilhelm I's warrant in 1862 (he was later crowned as German Emperor at Versailles in 1871).

Norton is now owned by Patrick Grant; with John Kent as their head cutter (formerly on his own in Stratton Street), they now make – very, very well, it must be said – for, amongst others, HRH the Duke of Edinburgh who is (if I may say so) always superbly turned out (even with the perennial handkerchief in his breast pocket!).

Norton & Sons now build clothes for, amongst others, European royal families and heads and former heads of state. They also have a strong reputation in country and sporting clothes. Although Norton & Sons are renowned for the types of clothing just described, they also build town and formal wear, like the firms more generally mentioned later in this chapter and in chapters 4, 5 and 7.

A.J. Hewitt bought out tropical tailor and outfitter Airey & Wheeler in 1998. Lord Carnarvon had been dressed by Henry Poole when he opened Tutankhamun's tomb. Apart from these makers, if

Norton were there on 10 November 1871 when Dr Livingstone was famously encountered by Sir Henry Morton Stanley at Ujiji on the banks of Lake Tanganyika – because they suited Stanley, with his 'unlimited expenses' from the *New York Herald*, for this expedition. Henry Poole lays *some* claim to Dr Livingstone and Cording's lays claim to *some* of Stanley's general gear for this particular expedition. Gieves & Hawkes also say that they kitted both of them out at some time during their African adventures.

Other famous Norton customers include the Marquis de Vogue (who, amongst other things, 'found' Russian writer Fyodor Dostoevsky for a French readership); A.J. Drexel Biddle, Jr (American diplomat); Sir Wilfred Thesiger (soldier, explorer, photographer and writer).

you want an actual explorer or safari suit, you might try Connock & Lockie.

However, if you are on a serious economy drive for this outfit, you might try an army surplus store. Sometimes they have stone-coloured tropical tunics and trousers for a few pounds and they are quite adequate for bush and savannah wear (they are necessarily and unselfconsciously worn with a sola topee – see the hats chapter). Team these up with **W.S. Foster & Son, Henry Maxwell, G.J. Cleverley & Co.** or **Tricker's** full brogue heavy country shoes and a flywhisk.

Classic Norton & Sons blue suit coat in Super 120s worsted.

TOPCOATS AND MACS

Heavy top coat (town wear or beagling)

There is little alternative to bespoke for this item. I suggest having a black cashmere and wool mix cloth coat with the possibility of an astrakhan collar. However, I should go for a tight, thick herringbone weave material which is likely to be quite hard-wearing. The Duke of Windsor had such a coat for most of his adult life. A hundred years ago, a coat like this would also have had – at least – a musquash (*Ondatra zibethicus*) lining. Lord Castlerosse's had sable. This would now be both an extravagance and quite unnecessary, bearing in mind the combined effects of modern transport conditions, global warming, tropical island living and central heating – together with the fact that beagling days are likely to be few and far between.

I once heard of a woman who, about thirty years ago, wanted a sable coat but the prevailing public opinion meant that she would have been risking life and limb every time that she wore it outside. Therefore, in order to satisfy her desires and avoid sustaining actual bodily harm, she had a bespoke raincoat lined with best Russian blue sable at a cost of several tens of thousands of pounds. No doubt, both she and her furrier were equally happy with the result. The very finest Russian blue sable (*martes zibellina*) comes from the Barguzin Valley in Russia and that is also called Crown or Imperial sable from the fact that it had been reserved for the royal family of Russia. In fact, it is dark brown or black with silvery blue guard (i.e. outer) hairs.

Lightweight topcoat (town)

Once again, it really is worth the investment to have a topcoat which will last forever. You should have this in a black or dark grey herringbone weave, double-breasted or Chesterfield style – maybe, if you go for the double-breasted option, with the pardonable prettiness of a velvet collar. A century ago, you would also have had silk facings or *revers* on the lapels but this, today, would be too noticeable to be passable, except on a bookie's runner or one of the sleazier politicians (and what a choice there is there). This coat would be very useful for late autumn and early winter days. Cording's famous (ready-made) covert coat is often worn around town as a lightweight topcoat in early spring and late autumn.

Mackintosh

You could go bespoke on this but since there is **Burberry**, there probably is no need. Because of its association with flashers in the park, this can be a slightly dubious item and it is difficult to avoid looking seedy when wearing it, although both Lord Peter Wimsey and Inspector Parker had one in Dorothy L. Sayers' Lord Peter Wimsey novels. Ian Fleming sometimes used to wear a light-weight blue mac even on aircraft journeys – even though it made him look like a spook. Accordingly, if you must have a mackintosh, I should go for a single-breasted *blue* Burberry; try to avoid the beige trenchcoat unless you really are off to the trenches because it tends to look rather Dick Tracy – but then you might *want* to look like Dick Tracy! However, I suggest that a riding mackintosh is

Burberry was founded by Thomas Burberry in Basingstoke in 1856. He invented gabardine waterproof cloth in 1880 and moved, in 1891, to the Haymarket where the headquarters remains. Burberry were outfitters to Roald Engelbregt Gravning Amundsen – who was the first man to reach the South Pole, in a race against Captain Robert Falcon Scott, and his famous team. They also supplied Sir Ernest Henry Shackleton, in his 1914 expedition to cross Antarctica.

permissible – and Cording's is the place to go for these – but they can get rather foetid inside since the rubber lining traps condensation (a sales pitch for them used to be: 'It streams both sides, sir!').

SOME FIRMS

Apart from those already mentioned old-established tailors (some described as 'Court Tailors and Breeches Makers') are Gieves & Hawkes (with the iconic address 1 Savile Row – the firm dates from the businesses of Hawkes in 1711 and Gieves in 1785) who also get a mention under formal dress and are first-rate all-round outfitters as well as tailors. There are also Davies & Son (who suited, amongst others, Lord Nelson (apparently sharing him with Gieves & Hawkes and 'Old Mel' Meredith), Sir Robert Peel, many European crowned heads in the Nineteenth and Twentieth Centuries (including their late Majesties Kings George V and Edward VIII) and their families, as well as Clark Gable, Joseph Kennedy, Tyrone Power, Douglas Fairbanks Jr (an actor also famous for denying being the headless man in a photograph showing Margaret, Duchess of Argyle, wearing only her pearls, smoking a cigar), Benny Goodman, and President Truman.

George Davies founded this firm in 1803 but, on his sudden death in 1804, it passed to his brother, Thomas. Formerly, they were in Hanover Street (where there was a royal fitting room set aside for King George V), and moved to Old Burlington Street in 1979. They have been in Savile Row since 1997. Subsumed in them now are the old firms of Wells, together with James & James and Johns & Pegg (where the great Frederick Scholte had been a cutter). The only blip in Davies & Son's history was the 'Scandal of the Duke of York's trousers'. It was reported in the press in 1892 that the trousers of the then Duke of York were made in a Soho sweatshop (used by the firm) where typhoid fever had broken out. The Duke of York later became King George V (in 1910), after the death of his elder brother. Despite the 'scandal', King George V remained a devoted Davies & Son customer!

Clark Gable with Hedy Lamarr in the film Comrade X: *photograph from the Everett Collection/Rex Features.*

There are also the tailors Henry Poole who founded Savile Row as *the* world centre of fine tailoring and who clothed many of the royalty and aristocracy of the world. This firm was established by James Poole in Bloomsbury in 1806 and gained a reputation as military tailors during the Napoleonic wars. They moved first to Regent Street in 1822 and then to 4 Old Burlington Street. In 1846

Cary Grant at the top of the tree: photograph from the Everett Collection/Rex Features.

Henry Poole owned the business and cut doors through into 32 Savile Row. It was rumoured that Henry Poole helped to finance the second French revolution of 1848 when King Louis Philippe was deposed by Louis Napoleon (later Emperor Napoleon III). In 1876 Henry Poole's cousin Samuel Cundey took over the firm. After that, at the height of bespoke tailoring in the Edwardian era, Henry Poole employed up to 14 cutters and 300 tailors, creating 12,000 bespoke items of clothing a year. They have held 40 royal warrants across Europe, the Middle East and Africa since 1858, as well as dressing other high-profile people. Around 1806, there had been other tailors in the vicinity of Savile Row – then largely a residential street: the more famous names are Weston, Schweitzer & Davidson, Adeney & Boutroy, John Levick, Stultz, John Meyer, and Burghart.

Henry Poole clothed Emperor Napoleon III (the last French Emperor) – who lived in exile for a while in King Street, St James's. Other famous customers were: Dr David Livingstone (Scottish missionary and explorer and the first European to discover the falls which he named the Victoria Falls), Charles Dickens, Anthony Trollope, Sir Winston Churchill and William Randolph Hearst (the original American newspaper tycoon whose life was, to his dismay, reflected in the film *Citizen Kane*).

Ede & Ravenscroft, established in 1689, are London's oldest tailors (and robe makers – they have made every sovereign's coronation robes, since the coronation of William and Mary in

1689). However, the name Ede & Ravenscroft dates from 1871 when Joseph Webb Ede married Rosanna Ravenscroft.

There are also Meyer & Mortimer (the original John Meyer, of Conduit Street, was one of Brummel's tailors) and **Dege (& Skinner)**, established in 1865 – who hold royal warrants from several royal houses. **H. Huntsman & Sons** (founded in 1849 in Albemarle Street and noted for sporting wear) is about the costliest. Kilgour, French & Stanbury is now abbreviated (since 2003), in the modern taste, to **Kilgour** and they can boast Cary Grant and Rex Harrison as former customers – as well as having made Fred Astaire's morning coat for the film *Top Hat*. Their origins trace back to T. & F. French (1882) which merged with A.H. Kilgour in 1923, taking in the Stanbury brothers in 1925.

There is **Bernard Weatherill**, founded by the father of the former Speaker of the House of Commons, which is justly famous for sporting and equestrian wear – they are now formally amalgamated with Kilgour. **Welsh & Jefferies** are tailors to Eton College. Connock & Lockie in Lamb's Conduit Street are not only well established and very skilled but cheaper than Savile Row. When I first knew them in 1978, they were in New Oxford Street; they then moved to the Sicilian Avenue and then to their current shop. Traditionalists pronounce Lamb's Conduit Street as Lamb's *Cundit* Street – and the road down to which it runs (Theobald's Road) as *Tibbald's* Road. Connock & Lockie have always had the splendid military pattern riding breeches and the big stag's head on display.

Timothy Everest, who trained with Tommy Nutter, is in Spitalfields and brings a contemporary twist to his work. He also offers made to measure and off the peg.

There is the business of **Douglas Hayward** in Mount Street; famed for dressing stars as diverse as Noel Coward and Michael Caine. The firm of **Hardy Amies** is also still in business, under creative director Ian Garlant, at 14 Savile Row. Here one can expect an individual style for bespoke and the very latest fashion in the couture ranges. Everything is still done in accordance with the spirit of Hardy Amies' own personal *dictum* at the head of this chapter.

Cutting, building and fitting

Any good tailor will consider, from the outset, that he is going to *build* you a suit, or a coat – or whatever else you bespeak. Just like any worthwhile construction, this is going to take time; longest the first time – but always some time. Wherever you go, you should normally get three fittings for fully bespoke clothes.

Although practices vary, often it is best to make an appointment. You might be asked who introduced you; although gone are the days when it was necessary to be introduced by a family member or another existing customer to get through the door. However, you may well see old copies of *Burke's Peerage* lying around, gathering dust, since the days when customers were vetted.

My first attendance at Davies & Son in about 1986 was after I had wandered around for long enough to have decided which cut of coat displayed in the various windows I thought the best for my young frame. I was greeted very politely by the benignly inquiring face of Mr Matthews, my cutter-to-be, who discreetly looked me up and down. I was wearing a shiny, old, dark-grey suit, off the peg years before, which plainly had not come from any near competitor of Davies & Son. The only thing that he said about this later was that the material was 'a little bit skimped' – you will find that every Savile Row tailor will always build in 'fullness' to avoid any possible appearance of 'skimping'. This saved my feelings and when he asked me what was my introduction, I just replied with a straightforwardness that defused any remaining tension: 'your window'. I still recall what was in there: a beautifully cut jet-black, single-breasted dinner jacket with shawl collar and lapels (or *revers*) – i.e. the wholly rounded type without steps or peaks – which just said everything about the understated elegance which I could expect – and always received.

When attending the appointment, the next stage is the measuring, which is done by the cutter of the cloth. He will also ask you whether your shirt and shoes are your usual types. This is so that the coat collar will sit properly and so that the trousers will fall away neatly onto the top of your shoes. His striker or under-cutter or even a front-of-house man will mark around 21 body measurements down on a special form, as the cutter calls them out, also noting (in a kind of discreet code) any asymmetries and idiosyncrasies – such as a drop on a shoulder, sloping or narrow shoulders, prominent calves and any other humps and bumps. Hold yourself naturally; there is no point in trying to appear a hero to your tailor – anymore than to your valet – not least because you are not going to stand normally with a ramrod back and with your stomach pulled in.

'No man is a hero to his valet' was an aphorism of Anne Bigot de Cornuel (1605–94) – worked over by many, including the dialectic logician Georg Wilhelm Friedrich Hegel, who explained: 'No man is a hero to his valet. This is not because the hero is no hero, but because the valet is a valet.'

On this form will go your selection of bespoke requirements: such as whether double or single-breasted coat; number of coat buttons; whether any or all sleeve buttons are to undo; whether coat pockets are to be straight or sloping. Does sir want an extra smaller ticket pocket? What about a fob pocket in the waistband of the trousers? You will also say whether you want turn-ups on the trousers and maybe turned-back Brandenburg cuffs on the coat, and discuss the size of lapel buttonhole. You will need to specify whether you want to use braces or have side adjusters on the trousers ('Daks tops'). Most tailors will tell you that braces are best and they are probably right. If you opt for braces, you will find that the top of the back of the trousers will be cut high in a curve up from the sides and at the top will be a V-shaped indentation, on either side of which will be the back buttons. Whatever you choose, you will need to be sure that your trouser-ends just touch the top of your shoes, without a break or a fold.

Of course, at some point, you will choose the cloth and the lining material from a bewildering array of bundles and pattern books.

The cutter then goes away and cuts a paper pattern, which is normally done in one of two ways. The first is called 'pattern manipulation' and involves the use of a standard block pattern (which comes in various regular sizes) on which the customer's pattern is formed with adjustments, according to the peculiarities of his shape and measurements. The second main type is the 'drafting formula' approach when the whole pattern is made from scratch.

Once the cloth is cut and made up by the tailor, you will receive a card or a telephone call. The first fitting is called the skeletal baste fitting and occurs after the cutter has cut the cloth and given it to the tailor (often freelance workers) whose job is to fit all the pieces

---

There are several books on the subject of pattern cutting, some of them running into many editions. One still referred to frequently around the Row is *The Sectional System of Gentleman's Garment Cutting: Comprising Coats, Vests, Breeches and Trousers &c* by J.P. Thornton, published by Minister & Co. I have seen a 2nd (new and enlarged) edn of this, dated 1894. There is also another book by Thornton, with the variation 'International System' which ran into many editions. J.P. Thornton was editor of *Minister's Gazette*, a director and teacher of Minister's Cutting Academy and a gold medallist and honorary member of the Parisian Inventor's Academy.

These books are still referred to – especially for items which are not frequently made, such as fur-covered shawl collars on winter top coats – and contain just about every pattern which is ever likely to be needed. Although things like frock coats and evening breeches are seldom made now, the knowledge of exactly how to make them is preserved here forever in these tailors' bibles. The idea of exactly what things should be and *how* they should be is infinitely more precious than owning a complete wardrobe of clothes (however enjoyable that might be). The books themselves include illustrations of the patterns, descriptions of them and pictures of examples of the finished items.

together using a floating canvas on the coat (i.e. a canvas base which is stitched but not stuck or fused to the material). Off-the-peg suits normally have the cheaper and more rigid fused canvas (which sometimes melts in dry-cleaning). Waiting for the appearance of the first draft of the suit is normally the longest wait. The clothes turn up with a paper ticket pinned to the sleeve, showing whose garment it is and the tailor's name. The customer is fitted with the suit, which has no collar at this time, and the cutter walks around, tugging and straightening, pushing your arms up and bending the elbows, making adjustments and markings with pins and chalk – sometimes after the frightening sound of rending of threads. On a single-breasted coat, the cutter will probably pull out the front and turn the two edges outermost to make sure that the material and the sit do not look 'skimped' – this is your breathing space – and a little room for the odd indulgence at table. After all, if you are to look as though you had forgotten all about your clothes after you put them on, you do not want to look as though you have been strapped in, holding your breath.

The next fitting, a few weeks later, is the forward fitting; according to the adjustments made. Tweaking of such matters as the sit of the shoulders is marked up. A few weeks later again and the customer gets the finish bar finish fitting – and after this, he should be able to walk out in the suit.

Remember that any good suit has a chassis and much can be achieved to amplify the good and to hide the defective, by padding, pinching, darting and stuffing – especially around the shoulders and waist. Kilgour and Hawes & Curtis (tailoring, now with Cording's) used to add extra padding to Cary Grant's shoulders to bring his large neck and head into better proportion with the rest. Grant, in turn, used to measure his new suits (and his shirts) with a rule and insist on alterations for even minute discrepancies. Hawes & Curtis used to undertake an exercise in padding to disguise Robert Donat's sloping shoulders. They also clothed the more symmetrical Jack Buchanan.

There are tailors who will cut you 'hard' or 'soft' coats; the difference being in the sharpness and rigidity of the shape: for

Jack Buchanan immaculately turned out in a town suit. This image used to hang in the foyer of the Garrick Theatre; it is now in the royal retiring room: photograph by Baron/Getty Images.

example, Anderson & Sheppard, also **Thomas Mahon** and **Steven Hitchcock** (separate businesses and both apprenticed with A & S) are renowned for the soft approach and, say, Huntsman, Dege or Davies & Son for the firmer (more military) shell. The best way to build an appreciation of the difference is to go around and see examples of the work of the various houses. Often they have window displays of recent work.

Some people use different tailors for coats and waistcoats, on the one hand, and trousers, on the other. Dating from the time of his governorship of the Bahamas during the Second World War, the late Duke of Windsor famously used to have his trousers (or 'pants') made in the USA, by a London-trained New York tailor, called H. Harris – although he continued to have his coats made in London (by such as Davies & Son and Frederick Scholte). The Duchess of Windsor ('one can never be too thin or too rich') called this 'pants across the sea'. However, if you choose this option, be careful that the cloth for the whole rig comes from the same or an identical bundle because even cloths subject to the same processes in manufacture (and supposed to be the same weave, weight and colour) can turn out with noticeable differences in colour if they come from different bundles.

Richard James offers suits which are cut in London but assembled abroad. You do not get three fittings but, if your dimensions and symmetry are normal, the saving on fully bespoke suiting is considerable and the product is Savile Row to all modern intents and purposes.

Then, of course, there are the modernists – such as **Ozwald Boateng** who generally cuts his coats rather long, sometimes in bright colours, and achieves a kind of smart, expensive Teddy Boy effect for the younger crowd.

There is also a firm called **Costello** in Ilford, Essex (of all places), which has built a deserved reputation not only as civilian tailors but also as military tailors and as film and theatrical costumiers. It represents astonishingly good value for money and provides excellent quality.

Giorgio Armani, well beloved of Frasier and Niles Crane (and every other *parvenu* on the planet), has opened an offensive against Savile Row; describing it, in an interview in the *Sunday Times* (9 July 2006) as 'a comedy, a melodrama lost in the past'. Perhaps he ought to make up his mind which he means because, as it stands, his verdict is contradictory. Armani's *fatto a mano su misura* (hand-made to measure) is soon to be launched in London and Milan before (as the interviewer puts it), *spreading* to New York, Tokyo and Los Angeles. Giorgio says, tellingly, 'Men need couture just as women do – something made exclusively for them to *define their social position*.' The emphasis in the quotation is my own.

Of course, normally, the clothing should reflect the social position, rather than define or create it; although heaven knows that

Englishman Ronald Colman and Kay Francis (a leading lady who, in the 1930s, was the highest paid film star), in a publicity poster for the 1930 film Raffles. *Armani must have overlooked this old black and white film: photograph by SNAP/Rex Features.*

there are those there who will jump at the ostensible opportunities offered by Armani's services – but it will not come cheap. The starting price will be £5,000 but it could rise to £30,000: 'if the customer wants a particularly luxurious, rare fabric, say a double cashmere with a particular wash, and a specially dyed silk lining he can have it – provided he can afford it' boasts Giorgio. Alternatively, I suggest, the customer could take a first-class return to the Orient; have a cloth woven in silk and cashmere mix (with his initials discreetly appearing in the weave), have the lining silk dyed with a rare vintage port, then have the suit made up fully bespoke in Savile Row – and still have plenty of change from £30,000. Mind you, he would not get the irresistible option of the matching croc handbag, watchstrap and shoes; taking the total, for one complete outfit, up to around £75,000. Armani scoffs that seeing someone in traditional Savile Row suiting is like looking at someone 'in an old English black and white film'. For my part, I would rather look like Clive Brook, Douglas Fairbanks (Sr or Jr), Ronald Colman, Cary Grant or Ray Milland than any of the modern 'celebrities' whom he will suit.

THE MADE TO MEASURE AND READY-MADE OPTIONS

New & Lingwood do nice lines in ready-made light-weight suiting: they use good material, it is sharply cut and nicely fitted; every part of the suit, including the trouser and sleeve lengths are just so on me and it really does take quite a careful inspection to discern that they are off the peg. They even have bright silk linings. The most obvious giveaway is the fact that the buttonholes are machine stitched (they are too thin and too even). However, bearing in mind that these suits outside the sales are about a fifth of the price of going bespoke (and down to a tenth in the sales), the overall advantage to the less fastidious is plain enough, although it is fair to say that they will probably not have the longevity of bespoke suiting.

There are a couple of other places which are renowned for first-rate, ready-made suiting: **Chester Barrie** and **Brioni** (famous for figging out the Brosnan James Bond). Of course, Brioni also does bespoke suiting and Chester Barrie's forte is off the peg (and made to measure). Although, in comparison with the *normal* cost of bespoke suiting in the environs of Savile Row, you are looking at between one half and one third of the price for ready-made or made to measure, these places are certainly not cheap. Indeed, the cost does not compare at all favourably with that of fully bespoke suiting at Steven Hitchcock or Connock & Lockie and it is around twice the cost of a fully bespoke suit at somewhere like Costello & Sons in Ilford.

As I end this chapter, I ought to mention a photograph of Hugh Cecil Lowther, the 5th Earl of Lonsdale (known as the Yellow Earl because, according to *Time* magazine for 18 June 1934, 'Yellow are the racing colours, the motor cars and the silk hats of footmen in the service of the Yellow Earl, Britain's beloved sporting peer the Earl of Lonsdale'). Taken at Brooklands in the twilight years between the wars, he was wearing a chalkstripe-patterned suit with a coat in similar shape to a morning coat (but with a step collar and two buttons on the coat), separate plain waistcoat and turn-ups on the trousers. He topped it off with a gardenia, a Coke hat and a cigar, and seemed to be having, in his own favourite phrase, 'lovely fun'. This shows that it was just a mixture of comfort, convenience and chance which gave us what have become the standard shapes of the modern lounge suit. There is no reason why the 'Lonsdale' style just described would strictly be less correctly worn in the same place today.

The Yellow Earl having 'lovely fun': photograph by Topical Press Agency/Getty Images.

Chapter Three

General Day Wear: Shoes

'Ee ain't no blooming 'tec – ee's a gentleman – look at his boots!' (Covent Garden porter's comment, about Professor Higgins' appearance, in *Pygmalion*, by George Bernard Shaw)

I KNOW that, in the Introduction to this book, I quoted Sir Arthur Quiller-Couch's opinion that it's the trousers that make the gentleman but there are those who would argue that going further than bespoke suits, coats and shirts and adding to the wardrobe even a small, but carefully chosen, selection of bespoke shoes will transform a very well-clothed man into a very *well-dressed* man. However, there is a wide range of excellent ready-made shoes too and they are also covered here.

BESPOKE SHOES

George Hoby 'The Great' who made boots for Brummell and who actually invented the original campaign Wellington boot, for the Iron Duke's military campaigns, is departed from St James's Street and Bond Street. Once when a customer complained that his Hoby top boots had split, according to the book *The Last Shall Be First*, by Brian Dobbs, he exclaimed: 'Good God! You've been walking in them!'

The Wellington campaign boot was in fact an adaptation of the Eighteenth-Century Hessian boot (originally from Hesse in Germany) which was a knee-length leather boot with tassels at the top of the front (as demonstrated in the photograph of the Brummell statue in the Introduction). Blüchers were half boots, named after another military figure: Field-Marshal von Blücher, Prince of

Wahlstatt (1742–1819). George Hoby II suffered damage to his shop, caused by an accident in the fog, on 4 December 1837; reported in *The Times* the next day: the Hastings branch coach, having just left the Old White Horse Cellar, in endeavouring to turn from Piccadilly into St James' Street 'ran into Hoby's shop window on the western corner which it demolished with a fearful crash, breaking upwards of 40 squares of glass'.

Old Man Thomas (who threw the job-seeking, young John Lobb out of his St James' Street shop, the young Lobb brandishing a horny Cornish fist and shouting as he left – prophetically – that he would build a firm that would see Thomas's off) is also gone.

John Lobb had been a poor Cornish labourer. One of his feet was injured and deformed in an accident and so, in order to get a pair of shoes that would accommodate him, he became a shoe-maker. Legend has it that his apprentice-piece is in Fowey Museum, Cornwall, near to his native village of Tywardreath. An apprentice-piece was usually a small-scale boot or shoe, which an apprentice was required to produce to demonstrate his accomplishment and so to justify the successful end of his apprenticeship. Most of the shoe-makers' shops have examples in cabinets: Poulsen Skone (at New & Lingwood) have a miniature top boot, which is a marvel to behold, with tiny stitches to attach the sole to the welt; goodness knows how many to the inch. Each stitch is represented by an indent, produced by serrating or *gimping* the leather to give a saw-tooth edge to the exposed part of the welt around the shoe (effectively, the protruding part of the sole, visible in a bird's eye view).

Ancient and venerable Henry Maxwell's (now with W.S. Foster & Son) were founded in 1750 as spur makers. From spurs it was a natural progression to their famous and superb riding boots (including cavalry boots) and then other footwear. They once had shops in London and Paris and, from the time of George IV, have held many royal warrants.

The present W.S. Foster & Son was established by Charles Chester in 1840. However, during an air raid in the Second World War, the Chester premises near Waterloo were bombed out and the firm moved in with Mrs Foster in Eagle Place, St James' because her

Fine examples of W.S. Foster & Son and Henry Maxwell bespoke work, sun-bleached punch-cap shoes.

husband had also been killed. The only thing that the then Mr Chester had salvaged from the wreckage was a half-hundred-weight iron weight which is still in the current shop. Their head last-maker, Terry Moore, was trained with Peal & Co. (then the biggest, the oldest and certainly one of the best shoe-makers in the world). Peal & Co were founded in 1565 in Durham; they moved to Derby in 1765 and to Oxford Street, London, in 1791. In 1953 Peal & Co. bought out Bartley & Sons. and took over their sign board ('shingle') of a fox and boot. Peal & Co. closed its doors, after four hundred years, in 1965, and the fox and boot shingle devolved upon Foster's who still display it, hanging outside their shop in Jermyn Street. Peal lasts are also still kept by Foster & Son as points of reference in making lasts for boots and slippers. Foster's are renowned for the sun-bleached finishes on some of their work. This finish was a serendipitous find because a customer asked them to give his shoes the finish of 'those in the window' which, through time, had become naturally sun-bleached. Now, some other firms offer this too. Apparently, the brand name 'Peal & Co.' is still in use in the USA.

John Lobb's is very much in the public eye. Lobb's motto is the biblical, 'The last shall be first' (Matt. 20: 16). The original John

Lobb received his first royal warrant (from the then Prince of Wales on 12 October 1863) when he was still a tradesman in New South Wales. According to Brian Dobbs's book, John Lobb had obtained the Prince's foot measurements by getting some inside knowledge (goodness knows how from the other side of the world, when the only communications were by ship), made the Prince a pair of boots and sent them to him. The Prince was extremely pleased with them – and the rest really is history. Lobb's did not have an actual London presence until 1866 when they set up in Regent Street with an enormous (and very immodest) royal warrant over the door. There they prospered, winning medals in international exhibitions (such as the Paris Exhibition of 1900) for the excellence of their work. Later they moved to the corner of St James's Street and Bennett Street where they were bombed out in the Second World War. They then moved down to 9 St James' Street – where they remain – in what may be the most beautiful shop in the world.

G.J. Cleverley are also conscious of (and meeting the need) for publicity to advertise their superb craftsmanship, which often includes the chiselled toe. Although it certainly does not apply to their workmanship, the use of the word 'square' to describe someone as old-fashioned or fuddy-duddy possibly derives from a change in fashion (from square-toed shoes to rounded-toes shoes) – with anyone not following the new fashion

Rudolph Valentino at the door of his house, in a pair of co-respondent shoes: photograph by SNAP/Rex Features.

The inimitable Rex Harrison – always well suited and booted – here with Audrey Hepburn and Wilfred Hyde White in an early scene from the film My Fair Lady: *photograph from the Everett Collection/Rex Features.*

castigated by being called a 'square' or 'square-toed'.

George Cleverley set up on his own with two acolytes John Carnera and George Glasgow in Cork Street, now in the Royal Arcade off Bond Street (and then passed the business on to them after his death in harness aged 93 in 1991). Cleverley had been apprenticed at the famous old firm of Niklaus Tuczek which traded variously from Clifford Street and Jermyn Street and was eventually bought out by Lobb's in 1968. Cleverley worked at Tuczek's from 1920 to 1958 and his customers had included Rudolph Valentino, Winston Churchill, Edward G. Robinson, Humphrey Bogart, Clark Gable, Gloria Swanson and Rex Harrison.

Taylor's are still in Paddington Street, making bespoke shoes.

Paul Davies ('the London Shoemaker') is also

Bespoke work from the Cleverley workshop: black calf whole cut shoe, from Cleverley.

well trained and experienced and extremely good value for bespoke shoes. **Edward Green,** and **Crockett & Jones** do both bespoke and ready-made lines.

Tricker's (established in 1829) have a very good value bespoke line and also do good special orders on standard-size lasts. New & Lingwood (also at Eton and Cambridge for all their products) make bespoke shoes under the name of the old firm of Poulsen, Skone & Co.

Gaziano & Girling are quite new boys on the block in Northamptonshire – but they do a superb range of bespoke shoes and boots – into which they plainly put all their art and sole. They also supply ready-made shoes and undertake special orders on standard lasts. Their styles range from traditional to cutting-edge contemporary – but without the funny little quirks of **Berluti** (who put 'patches' on some of their contemporary lines).

I have to say that, unless you have very unusual feet, wear your shoes a lot softer than I do and you can afford many pairs, you may well be tempted go for one of the 'to go' options that are available as well as 'special orders'. I say this bearing in mind that, at the beginning of my career, when I was being measured for lasts in one bespoke establishment, the last-maker asked whether the pair of shoes that I was wearing was made by them; in fact the shoes were made 'to go' by a firm that I would not even now strongly recommend at all!

However, if it is got *just so*, the fit, lightness, durability and general form – especially the heels – of good bespoke shoes are worth the waiting (and paying) for. It is also to be remembered that the materials used in bespoke shoes are always better than the materials used in even excellent ready-made shoes. For example, the leather tanning is always done in the laborious and traditional way using immersion in an oak bark process (as opposed to the quicker modern process of chrome tanning). Moreover, the trees will fit perfectly because they will be copied off the last by a special machine.

Remember too that with bespoke shoes you can have everything done, within the art, as you want it done. This means that you are not stuck with having the usual very light-tan shoe linings that nearly always appear in ready-made shoes. Why not have a colour to match the outer shoe – or to contrast with it such as blue, green or post-box red? The shanks of bespoke shoes (the part between the sole and the heel) normally have a pleasing, rounded ('fiddle-back') finish. Here too you can specify the colour. It is usual for the soles, shanks and under-heels of bespoke shoes to be in a colour that matches the tops. Accordingly, you would have black to match black shoes and brown to match brown shoes. Ready-made shoes nearly always have a flat shank and the whole of the under-side is left in an unpleasing very light tan, which soon gets grubby.

If you are considering stepping out further afield, **Laszlo Vass** in

> You can avoid VAT with bunions or worse, *necessitating* bespoke footwear – or if you live outside the European Union. A word here on the paying front: many a wry smile has been raised by the story of the cavalry officer who ordered a pair of boots during the Second World War, to be asked politely whether he might yet be ready to pay for those that he had had in the First – but tailors and shoe-makers have just about caught up with the fact that they can sue you. Things are never going to be as they used to be: otherwise, the term 'ready-made' would just not appear in this work. However, you can generally expect a couple of months' free credit for bespoke clothing.

Budapest has a worldwide reputation with a matching international customer list, and claims to be able to produce shoes to match anything that London has to offer for a third of the price. His speciality is the 'Budapest' which is a sturdy full brogue Derby-style of shoe, described by him, as by Americans, as a 'wing-tip' Derby. In England we say 'full brogue' Derby for such a shoe – and 'half' or 'semi brogue' for the shoe with a simple tooled toe cap. A Derby is distinguished from an Oxford brogue in that the laces are set in a V-shaped front.

A handsome galosh-topped boot (shown here with ordinary, not shanked, buttons), from the Foster & Son and Henry Maxwell collection.

If you do take the bespoke route, consider a pair of black calf galosh-topped button boots or shoes, for formal morning occasions. You will not find these ready-made and not easily as a special order on a standard last. The main body of the shoe is cut like a pump and the tops are made of grey buckskin (or 'nubuck' which is really just processd calfskin), which normally fasten with strong, shanked mother-of-pearl buttons down the side. You will need a button hook and plenty of manual dexterity to get them securely into place – but you can be pretty sure that there will not be many others wherever you go.

Bespoke shoes require several individual craftsmen to make them and, in the middle of the Nineteenth Century, there were literally thousands of shoe-makers in London. The fitter does the measuring and drawing for the last-maker. The last is the wooden replica of the outline of the feet and is formed by the last-maker. It is this around which the shoes will be fashioned. This involves the customer standing on paper, which will form the pattern for the lasts. An outline of the feet is drawn and then measurements around the feet are taken and noted together with any peculiarities (I once saw the

Fred Astaire's shoe last from the Foster & Son and Henry Maxwell collection.

patterns and lasts of a king who was described on the pattern as 'hammer-toed'). The last-maker hand-forms the lasts out of beech and sometimes changes will need to be made to them because feet, like the rest of our parts, change in time. The last-maker hands on to the clicker who cuts the leather out for assembly around the lasts. The closer sews it all together and the maker adds the soles and heels. Finally, the polisher finishes the process off. Apart from the fitter and the last-maker (often the same person) there are often out-workers or freelance workers used in the shoe-making process.

TOWN SHOES

Always wear black calf or kid leather. There was a time when men wore patent leather in the daytime too but those days have gone and I am not going to suggest that they should return. So far as calf is concerned: there is waxed calf and box calf. The difference between them is that box calf is what is generally recognized as normal leather, whereas waxed calf is made with the suede side outermost, necessitating laborious blacking and polishing with a deer bone to make it shine. You will not readily get waxed calf unless you take the bespoke option. Waxed calf can be brought to a higher state of gleaming than box calf but at expense of time, patience and much effort.

On the buy-to-go front, I favour Green's 'Oxford' lace-ups with a single line of tooling around the toe cap and their 'Macmillan' 'Monk' style. W.S. Foster & Son, New & Lingwood and Cleverley also sell great ready-made lines. Berluti (established in 1895) make sharp Italian town shoes to go. Some Berluti ranges are definitely for the young and adventurous (edgy rather than spivvy, sometimes with heavily sun-bleached light-tan finishes, giving an antique look) and there is no doubting the craftsmanship in the products. They also offer a bespoke service. There are the well-known brands **Church's** and **Grenson's** – Grenson's still do bespoke and special orders on standard lasts. Their bespoke option is about a third of West End prices.

COUNTRY SHOES

These would be brown (light-weight) and all of the firms mentioned above do admirable ranges in half and full brogue styles. If you are having bespoke brown shoes the best leather is Russia leather (although not as expensive as crocodile) – and there is some available which was rescued after nearly 200 years at the bottom of the sea. In 1973 divers in Plymouth Sound found the wreck of a Dutch brigantine called the *Catherina von Flensburg* which had sunk there in a storm in 1786. On board were rolls of Russia leather (mainly reindeer hide). These were salvaged and treated in Cornwall and found to be in perfect condition. The precise formula for making true Russia leather was lost in the Russian Revolution. New & Lingwood as well as G.J. Cleverley (who was a consultant to Poulsen Skone at New & Lingwood) have a stock of this original material and you can bespeak shoes made out of it; smelling distinctively, as it does, of the birch oil used in its treatment. Other makers may also have it or be able to obtain it. The tanner's initials are still visible and the hatched grain created by stamps applied by hand is still present. They are also available from New & Lingwood ready-made for just under £1,000 a pair. You would not wear these in the field – more likely: to a morning service in a country church, for luncheon in a country inn, to support summer fetes in the rectory garden and similar events.

Chapter Four

Formal Morning Dress

W eeping may endure for a night, but joy cometh in the morning. (Psalms 30:5)

INTRODUCTION

THIS FIRST section deals with the proper formal morning dress for the usual occasions of weddings, royal garden parties, christenings and Royal Ascot. Very Formal Morning Dress is dealt with afterwards and is mainly of interest rather than of any practical use. More specific detail on appropriate hats is given in Chapter 8.

MORNING COAT

A morning coat is absolutely essential and should be single-breasted in black herringbone worsted, with formed cuffs (the top part of the cuffs are single-pleated parallel to the end of the sleeves) but with double-breasted-style peaked lapels, including a large buttonhole and tail pockets – that is to say, pockets in the linings of the tails, because there are no external pockets on this coat. Just like the swallow-tail evening coat, the tails should reach down to the back of

HSH Prince Alexander of Teck, 1st Earl of Athlone (1874–1957), in a morning coat with ribbon edging.

the knees. You can ask for ribbon braiding around the edges of the collar, lapels and down around the tails. Some suitable tailors to make all this up for you are listed in Chapter 2 on daywear. Despite negative commentaries, there is no reason why a bow tie (as long as it is obviously not an evening tie) may not be worn with a morning coat. Sir Winston Churchill sometimes used to wear a polka-dot-spotted bow tie with morning dress. If you have ribbon around one coat, you will need another for more formal occasions, such as formal City luncheons and breakfasts, without ribbon and, for such occasions, you will also need a waistcoat of the same material as the coat; preferably also with detachable white tabs around the inside of the V of the neckline. The procedure for sitting down in such a coat is identical with that for sitting down in an evening swallow-tail coat or a frock coat – that is to say, flip the tails up over the seat and do not divide the tails.

FROCK COAT

This is so-called because it is heavily waisted and slightly balloons out from the waist. If you have one of these, you will certainly stand out a little from the crowd, at weddings, christenings or funerals. It should be made in black (as for the morning coat, above) and be in double-breasted style with indented corded silk (*faille*) lapel facings (*revers*) and basket-weave silk buttons. However, beware of fancy long lounge suit coats, without the proper cut and detail, in wedding clothes shops (even in the gods' quad) – unless you really are a famous modern footballer. Sir Winston Churchill's son, Randolph, banked at Coutts & Co. in Old Park Lane where the manager wore a frock coat. Once, when the circumstances were dire and he urgently needed an increase in his overdraft, he too wore his frock coat to the interview – so as not to be at a disadvantage. Coutts & Co. managers no longer wear frock coats in modern Britain.

If you do wear your frock coat to a funeral, substitute black trousers (the Victorians often used their evening trousers) for the spongebag or hound's-tooth trousers. Again, I suggest that you ask for formed cuffs. Tail pockets are also necessary since, just like morning coats, this coat does not have external side pockets. This item can sometimes be had second hand but this is, obviously, very much potluck.

Having mentioned funerals, it must be said that, usually, these days, men wear a dark suit, white shirt and black – or at least dark – tie (with dark outer garments in the cold and wet) and black shoes – never wear, in the words of an old monologue; 'brown boots at a funeral'.

The procedure for sitting down in a frock coat is the same as that for a morning coat – you flip the tails up over the seat.

FORMAL MORNING SHIRTS

Always have a couple of white cotton or linen day shirts with detachable stiff (fold-down) collars for formal day occasions (New & Lingwood do nice wide cutaway collars called the 'Cameron'). You will need the stiff collar to be half a size above the neckband of the shirt, which itself should be in your usual size. It is unusual now to wear stick-up collars, except with a stiff evening shirt or with robes if you are a judge or barrister. A hundred years, or so, ago, stiff stick-up collars were worn with morning dress but the shirts themselves were as stiff around the cuffs as their evening

The archaic garb of judges and barristers is drawn from different periods. The gowns and clerical bands are medieval – although, specifically, *black* gowns from when the court went into mourning for King James I – the wigs and court dress are Eighteenth Century, the collars are Victorian. One of the recent Lord Chancellors, for some unknown reason, abolished the use of mourning bands and 'weepers' for periods of court mourning. Mourning bands were edged black and 'weepers' were lace cuffs worn by Her Majesty's Judges and Counsel with full legal court dress (presumably, to wipe away the notional tears).

Ernest Beckett MP (1856–1917) in a frock coat, buff waistcoat and spongebag trousers.

counterparts (how else did Sherlock Holmes use his cuffs as notepads?).

If you are taking the bespoke option, you can go for several detachable soft collars as alternatives on these shirts. You could even have surgeon's (detachable) cuffs – so called because surgeons could remove them when operating (and so avoid splashes of blood) – to get the most out of a fairly hefty investment, but be aware that braces tend to wear the yoke and front of shirts anyway and detachable parts can be unnecessarily time-consuming. Moreover, the parts are apt, like socks, to go missing in the laundry.

You will need a good grey woven silk tie to wear with formal morning dress. However, people often wear a brightly coloured woven silk tie these days; especially to social events, such as Royal Ascot.

FORMAL WHITE DAY WAISTCOATS

Have a couple of these in single-breasted white woollen worsted or linen, with lapels and shanked mother of pearl buttons (shanked buttons are those with the top of the button in an unperforated roundel of shell and attached to the material by thread through a metal loop (the shank) which is stuck onto the back of the button) – white is very much smarter than grey or beige. However, it is also correct to have the same material as the morning or frock coat, perhaps with white edging around the lapels; very *sportif*. Tailors, like Americans, call waistcoats 'vests' (hence, I suppose, 'under-vests' – with which, I regret, I do not deal at all).

FORMAL MORNING CASHMERE SPONGEBAG TROUSERS

These are so-called because the patterns resemble striped spongebags. I suggest having one pair (in detail they should be the same as the hound's-tooth trousers). These are mainly for more formal day occasions such as City luncheons. Although the Edwardians do seem, sometimes, to have turned up even formal morning trousers, these do not now have turn-ups.

MORNING SMALL PATTERN HOUND'S-TOOTH TROUSERS

Have one pair, plain *without cuffs*, as a dashing alternative to formal morning striped sponge-bag cashmere formal trousers. However, although you could very properly wear these to a wedding or to Royal Ascot, you should really not wear them to very formal functions, such as City luncheons as they look a little 'fast' in such environments. The Victorians and Edwardians often wore light grey or buff trousers with morning dress. Mr Justice Byles, a Nineteenth-Century Judge, once remonstrated with Counsel (who would later become a Lord Chief Justice of England): 'Mr Coleridge, I have very little pleasure in listening to the arguments of Counsel whose legs are encased in light grey trousers.'

FORMAL SHOES OR BOOTS

The detail of these is dealt with under town shoes in Chapter 3: in short, have either galosh-topped shoes or boots (necessarily bespoke) or plain black Oxfords with toe caps (either bespoke or ready-made, which might have a single line of tooling across the band of the toe cap).

LEMON CHAMOIS GLOVES

Amazingly, these are still available – from Pickett and **Chester Jefferies** (but for how much longer?). They are correct for formal morning wear. They should fit like a second skin when *worn* at all. These can be washed by hand with soft soap (such as 'Lux') and stretched

A pair of chamois gloves – unusual these days, but perfectly correct.

out to dry naturally – but neither gloves nor ties are really quite the same after cleaning, however carefully it is done.

VERY FORMAL MORNING WEAR

For very formal morning wear, if you have no naval or military uniform, at City luncheons or for meeting Her Majesty outside a court audience setting, wear the morning coat without the ribbon edging, similar coloured waistcoat (with detachable white edging around the neck) and spongebag cashmere trousers with no buttonhole flower (certainly not a buttonhole flower with decorations) and never have a display handkerchief. Have a white shirt, stiff collar and woven grey silk tie with plain black oxfords or galosh-topped shoes or boots, chamois gloves and black topper.

These days, ambassadors wear full evening dress, rather than proper court dress (complete with oak leaf bullion), described below, when presenting their credentials to court and at the State Opening of Parliament (which are day events). Since civilian court dress (also briefly described below) used to be worn, by civilians, for investitures, I suppose that, logically, now white tie would be appropriate for these too – at any time of day.

This seems to be supported by the 'Alternative Court Dress' referred to in pronouncements of the Lord Chamberlain's Office that the King had approved alternative court dress in, for example, 1914 and 1920 (see e.g. the *London Gazette* for 7 May 1920) and by the very similar 'new pattern cloth (alternative) Evening Dress' in the Army and Navy Stores' Catalogue for 1939. However, this alternative (introduced on grounds of economy) did not originally apply to members of the royal households or members of the diplomatic or consular services who were still required to wear their full uniforms.

The 1939 description of this rig (previously known as 'Frock dress') included full fig evening dress coat with silk facings. Gieves & Hawkes, famous for designing and making naval and military uniforms (around the world) as well as for Civil Service uniforms, started in naval Portsmouth well over 200 years ago. They say that

F.E. Smith in very formal morning dress for his maiden speech in the House of Commons; he did have a buttonhole – it was his maiden speech and he was F.E. Smith.

tailcoats of every kind originally derive from naval officers' coat patterns from 1748 onwards. As a matter of general interest, they dressed Admiral Lord Nelson, the Duke of Wellington, Captain Bligh (of the *Bounty*) and Captain 'Kiss me' Hardy.

The swallow-tail coat in this alternative evening dress rig goes with a white *or* dark waistcoat, black evening cloth or stockinette breeches, with three black cloth-covered buttons and a black strap and buckle at the knee (unlike evening trousers, with no braid down the side) and with black silk stockings (or 'hose') which would go under the knee ends of the breeches, black pumps with bows (rather than buckles), white dress shirt with stiff front and cuffs and stick up collar and white tie and white gloves. Before 1929, it also included an opera hat (at the beginning of the Twentieth Century, it had been a ribbed silk cocked hat – *chapeau bras* or arm hat). If you do have an opera hat, when else could you wear it? Accordingly, do so, since they have not actually been *proscribed*. Probably now the pragmatic would substitute full fig evening trousers for the breeches. It is not appropriate to wear to court occasions a buttonhole flower (and, as above, certainly not a buttonhole flower with decorations).

I cannot seriously believe that these notes and thoughts will persuade High Court Judges and Senior Civil Servants away from pitching up for their routine gongs in other than what they regard as 'safe' Moss Bros finest morning coats, double-breasted grey waistcoats and felt black toppers, hired by their staff – and even less get modern British television 'celebrities' up to sartorial snuff but, at least, here is set out how it should be done.

General civilian court dress had been, from the middle of Victoria's reign, variations on a black cutaway silk velvet coat and waistcoat (with gilt or steel buttons) – although sometimes the waistcoats were white satin – velvet breeches, white dress shirt, tie and gloves, black silk stockings, *chapeau bras* (unwearable ribbed silk or beaver cocked hat, for carrying only), dress sword and gilt or steel-buckled pumps. Sir (Henry) Rider Haggard, the colonial administrator and writer, received his KCBE in such a suit on 25 February 1919.

High Sheriffs still wear a version of this court dress on ceremonial

Sir Winston Churchill, in full evening dress with breeches and decorations; the outfit amounting to alternative court dress, outside 10 Downing Street, waiting for the Queen and the Duke of Edinburgh to arrive, for his farewell dinner as Prime Minister, on 4 April 1955. Lady Churchill is in the doorway: photograph from Rex Features.

occasions, frequently made by Henry Poole. The Office of High Sheriff of a county is the oldest secular office under the Crown and predates the Norman Conquest. Originally, the High Sheriffs exercised many delegated powers which are now vested in others: from High Court Judges to magistrates and the Inland Revenue.

By the time that Francis Chichester came to be knighted, after his historic solo circumnavigation of the globe, at Greenwich, on 7 July 1967 (with the sword with which Queen Elizabeth I had knighted Sir Francis Drake), he pitched up in a dark lounge suit. In fairness, it did happen *al fresco* and at Greenwich – but now we have folks turning up for investitures in open-necked shirts. Once latitude is allowed, it's a slippery slope.

The full court uniforms for ambassadors and governors-general were used down to the 1980s and comprised a black cloth swallow-tail coat, high to the neck and cut square to the front, embroidered with gold bullion (braid) in an oak leaf pattern, with black cloth breeches with gold piping (or trousers for levées) and silk stockings, buckled court pumps, a bicorne beaver cocked hat with swan plumes and a bullion loop, a dress sword and white gloves.

Levées were court events begun by the French 'Sun King', Louis XIV, who would receive courtiers in his bedchamber at his *rising*. Over the years, levées became formalized morning receptions. It is notable that the Prince Regent used to attend upon Beau Brummell at his toilette in his house in Chesterfield Street, Mayfair, to observe how the Master dressed. The Governor-General of Canada holds a levée on New Year's Day. Apart from that, they are now no longer arranged.

The latest version of the Lord Chamberlain's court dress coat (1st class) is illustrated, modelled on a privy counsellor's (or councillor's) uniform. '1st class' means, in practical terms, that the coat has a full five inches width of bullion (gold embroidery). The Lord Chamberlain is one of the senior members of the royal household. This coat was recently exhibited in Paris and demonstrates the art and skill plainly still plied in Savile Row.

Ede & Ravenscroft are famous for producing robes of all kinds: especially academic, legal and parliamentary and those for the sovereign and peers. Every year they still fig out the new influx of (a hundred or so) Her Majesty's Counsel (QCs) in their court coats and breeches, silk gowns and full-bottomed wigs for their induction, as well as providing a hire service of gowns and hoods and other academicals for the graduates of the ever-increasing number of universities. They are also the oldest established tailors in England and shirt-makers.

Chapter Five

Evening Dress: Both White Tie and Black Tie

C rime committed in evening dress is what most appeals to popular imagination. (Anatole France)

INTRODUCTION TO THIS TECHNICAL AREA

THERE is no doubt that most people look their best in evening dress or, more accurately, will look their best – if they get it right. There are two principal kinds of civilian evening dress in the modern world. These are commonly called 'white tie' (otherwise known as 'full evening dress' or 'full fig') and 'black tie' (otherwise just called 'dinner jacket' or 'DJ'). The DJ is called a 'tuxedo' or 'tux' in some parts of America and Ireland. On much of the European continent and in Latin America it is called a 'smoking'. There is also the actual velvet smoking suit for the host to wear at private dinner parties at home – and, of course, for smoking in.

Before describing the various outfits in detail, it may be interesting to note some of the places where they are still worn. Events requiring *white tie* are few and far between. However, there are some still. One such occasion is being called to the Bar by Gray's Inn and 'published an Utter Barrister' – which sounds close to *Private Eye*'s opinion of lawyers in general. Then, of course, there are some balls which still require it and it is worn at dinners in the City of London, notably at City Livery Companies. These are trade guilds originally founded to promote the various skilled trades. They have – or share – magnificent premises, including banqueting halls.

Dinners at the Guildhall are also still 'white tie'. Once, in certain circles, white tie was worn to any evening event at which ladies were present and black tie was reserved for home, hotels abroad and stag dos.

Nowadays, events at which evening dress is worn usually have

Jack Buchanan (left) and Fred Astaire in full fig – including toppers and malacca canes in the number 'I guess I'll have to change my plan' from the film The Band Wagon: *photograph from the Everett Collection/Rex Features.*

invitations or tickets on which will be specified the dress code for the event. Frequently, this is 'black tie'. Such events will include some social association and club dinners and balls and some university balls and alumni events, professional association events and some private dinner parties.

The *white tie* is worn with a starched, stiff-fronted evening shirt (the stiffness results from the application of starch – starching has to be done professionally and I recommend the **Mayfair Laundry**) and wing collar, (normally) a white waistcoat, a swallow-tail evening coat and trousers, with silk half hose (avoiding *mezza calza*) and evening pumps.

Black tie is now normally worn with a soft-fronted evening shirt with a fold-down collar. Over this goes the dinner jacket and trousers and it is finished off with silk half hose, evening shoes or evening pumps. With single-breasted DJs a waistcoat or cummerbund is also worn.

There are some variations on the two themes and these are described in detail below.

WHITE TIE – SWALLOW-TAIL EVENING COAT AND TROUSERS

The swallow-tail evening coat has survived (just) from the standard pattern of coat worn all the time in the early Nineteenth Century. This has a cutaway front so that the coat stops at the waist in the front but it has tails exactly down to the back of the knee.

When sitting in a coat with tails, do *not* divide them (as King George IV said of Prime Minister Sir Robert Peel: 'He is no gentleman, he divides his coat tails!') but flip them up over the seat.

Raffles, 'gentleman thief' in the novels of E.W. Hornung, probably wore a swallow-tail evening coat in midnight blue vicuña/silk mix (*Vicugna vicugna*, a small South American camel, produces the finest wool; other suitable cloths include cashmere, merino or lamb's wool barathea).

One should have a silk velvet collar, corded silk (otherwise called silk *faille*) lapel facings (otherwise called *revers*). Satin, a warp-dominant silk weave, is the modern alternative to corded silk but is, to my mind, rather too shiny. The usual lapel pattern is the peaked style, familiar from double-breasted coats. If this style is adopted, it is very smart to have recessed facings; so that the silk is framed by the woollen material. The other acceptable style is the fully rounded shawl collar and lapels. Insist on a large buttonhole (to accommodate a gardenia, camellia or white carnation), silk-covered buttons and have tail pockets – since these coats have no external pockets and just two inside breast pockets.

Some say that black velvet collars were introduced onto coats as marks of mourning for victims of Madame Guillotine, during the French Revolution. Obviously if your coat is midnight blue, matching blue velvet is probably more appropriate; although the Duke of Windsor's midnight blue swallow-tail coat had black silk facings (and no obvious velvet).

The entertainer Jack Buchanan most certainly often wore full fig in midnight blue and stood out on stage and screen

Duke of Windsor's full fig: still a classic design. This puts to bed for all time the question whether a dark waistcoat may be a proper part of this outfit. The outfit, the gift of the Duchess of Windsor, is in the Metropolitan Museum of Art in New York, which owns the copyright in the photograph.

from the other men who wore black. Moreover, it is a curious feature that midnight blue can look almost darker than black – certainly richer and deeper, especially by candlelight.

The cloth merchants Loro Piana in Bond Street exclusively supply vicuña but when I last inquired they had blues only in pinstripes.

Except for liveried footmen, it is virtually unknown now for this coat to be worn with breeches and silk stockings; two hundred years

It was a while before the new pantaloons caught on *everywhere*: Almack's was a set of grand rooms established by one William Macall in February 1765 in King Street, which connects St James's Street and St James's Square. Entrance to the exclusive and much sought after Wednesday Balls was by ticket only and these were whimsically dispensed by Lady Patronesses, who acted in rotation. The point of the balls was to be noticed; it certainly was not to drink, because only soft drinks were supplied, and it certainly was not to eat excessively, because the fare largely comprised thin buttered bread and dry cake. The dances were initially Scotch reels and country dances. In around 1813 the French Quadrille was introduced. The illustrious Duke of Wellington (although a season ticket-holder) was once turned away because he was seven minutes late (the doors closed at 11 pm sharp) and wearing the new pantaloons and not the prescribed breeches. His request for admittance was relayed to the leading light of London Society, Lady Jersey, who sent the reply: 'Give my compliments to the Duke of Wellington and say that she (i.e. Lady Jersey) is very glad that the first enforcement of the rule of exclusion is such that hereafter no one can complain of its application.' (Presumably this was after 11 May 1814 when he was created Duke of Wellington.) According to engravings of the period, by about 1815, pantaloons and trousers had begun to supersede breeches and now, nearly 200 years later, most would not dare to wear evening breeches at all.

after Brummell first introduced pantaloon trousers for evening wear. Evening breeches are still correct and might be worn with a hunting scarlet swallow-tail coat to a hunt ball (assuming that one is entitled to hunting scarlet).

The stockings are worn underneath the knee-end of evening breeches (as they used to be with court breeches). The last person credibly to wear evening breeches in public was probably Sir Winston Churchill when he gave his farewell dinner, as PM, for HM the Queen and HRH The Duke of Edinburgh, on 4 April 1955 (as his friend, F.E. Smith, said: 'Winston can make do with the best of everything').

Breeches should still be worn for Garter ceremonies. However, it is clear from press photographs that they do not seem to be worn for these anymore and the stocking garter is worn over the *trousers* above the left knee. This is truly a ridiculous consequence of half-hearted attempts by courtiers at a public demonstration of a social egalitarianism which will never really exist.

On occasions when (royal) court dress was once worn, white tie (rather than morning dress) is now substituted, even for day events (e.g. by foreign ambassadors at the State Opening of Parliament).

The trousers should have a *double* stripe of silk braid down the side. *None* of this outfit should appear in *brown*.

A hunting scarlet evening coat in the making, by Norton & Sons – it will have indented lapel facings in buff faille.

The Most Noble Order of the Garter is the principal English Order of Chivalry or Knighthood. The Order comprises no more than 25 full members: Knights or Ladies Companion plus the Sovereign and Supernumeraries who may include foreign Sovereigns. The Order was probably founded by Edward III after an incident at Eltham Palace. He was dancing with the then Countess of Salisbury when her stocking garter fell to the floor – to the merriment of the other dancers. The King took the garter and placed it on his own leg, declaring: 'Honi soit qui mal y pense' – Norman French for 'shame be upon him who thinks ill of it'. A ceremonial garter is still worn by members of the Order and it bears the phrase as the motto of the Order. The main ceremony is a service in St George's Chapel, Windsor (now held in Ascot week). This service was revived by George VI (reigned 1936–52). The Knights and Ladies process in their robes, gongs, velvet caps with ostrich plumes and their garters to the Chapel from the Castle and the service is performed; any new Knights or Ladies also being installed. They then return to the Castle by carriage – presumably for a banquet, when they *might* be able to say: 'There's an ostrich feather in my soup.'.

Waistcoat

Make sure that your waistcoats are made by somebody who has seen you in the coat because it is *absolutely vital* that the waistcoats should not protrude from beneath the sides of the front of the coat.

Have, say, two waistcoats made in the same cloth as the coat (these used to be for winter wear and for periods of Court Mourning) and a couple made in the same Marcella as your stiff-fronted evening shirts (these waistcoats would once have been London summer wear). As will be remembered, from Chapter 4, white tie and dark waistcoat or white waistcoat with full fig was sanctioned by the (royal) court as part of alternative court dress.

As described above, it is a misconception that only a butler or *maitre d'* would ever wear a dark waistcoat with a swallow-tail evening coat; although *he* would probably wear a black tie with it. A *black tie* is worn with a swallow-tail evening coat *only* by servants, waiters, stewards and beadles.

The dark waistcoat option with full fig is perfectly demonstrated by the above picture of one of the late Duke of Windsor's full evening dress outfits on display at the Metropolitan Museum of Art in New York. The midnight blue coat and waistcoat were made in 1938 by Frederick Scholte of London and the trousers were replacements made by H. Harris (a London-trained New York-based tailor) in 1965.

DINNER JACKET AND TROUSERS

Black tie and dinner jacket began its vogue for stag dos, no doubt mimicking mess and wardroom. People generally refer to 'black tie' as denoting dinner jacket and black tie – but a dinner jacket may be (virtually) any colour; black or midnight blue is usual but Noel Coward had *brown* ones (made by Douglas Hayward, tailor to the stars), worn, with matching tie and pumps, by Coward right up until his last public appearance.

An example of one of Coward's brown dinner jackets is now to be seen in the Theatre Collection of the Metropolitan Museum of the City of New York (and a pair of his monogrammed slippers – made by Tricker's – is in the Theatre Museum in Covent Garden, along with a dressing gown). Therefore, I do not feel able to say that, although *most unusual*, even brown is *incorrect* for a dinner jacket. Presumably, he adopted it because brown is a warmer colour than black or blue for a stage performer and, anyway, he *was* Noel Coward. Nevertheless, I cannot positively recommend following him on this.

When Beau Brummell began the process which eventually led to monochrome evening dress, his evening coat was, according to Captain Jesse's account, blue, the waistcoat was white, his pantaloon trousers (from which we get the American 'pants') black

Life *magazine photograph of Noel Coward in the Las Vegas desert during a cabaret tour. He is wearing his brown dinner jacket outfit – note the errant, even extravagant, breast pocket handkerchief and the cigarette holder, which he did not generally use. (This holder conforms to the generally accepted rule that a man's cigarette holder should be no more than 4 inches long.) A DJ in the desert – Mad Dogs and Englishmen! Photograph by Loomis Dean/Getty Images (Time and Life Pictures Collection).*

and his stockings striped.

One should also have the dinner jacket and trousers in vicuña/silk mix as the ultimate (again, Loro Piana supplies the vicuña cloth); otherwise you can have cashmere or merino or plain lamb's wool barathea. I suggest that you opt for two-piece, single or double-breasted (in midnight blue or black).

It is worth noting that it was the Duke of Windsor who was one of the first, after the Victorian craving for black, to adopt, in the Twentieth Century, midnight blue as an alternative to black for evening dress. He also placed his *imprimatur* on double-breasted dinner jackets – with high, wide lapels to give an impression of a broader chest.

He explained his status in the fashion world in his book *A Family Album*:

> I was in fact 'produced' as a leader of fashion, with the clothiers as my showmen and the world as my audience. The middleman in this process was the photographer, employed not only by the Press but by the trade, whose task it was to photograph me on every possible occasion, public or private, with an especial eye for what I happened to be wearing.

As with the swallow-tail coat, have corded silk lapel facings and again insist on having a large buttonhole (for gardenia, camellia or *claret* clove carnation). Make sure that there is no fancy cuff-work and never have flaps on dinner jacket pockets and, strickly, also avoid back vents. The collar and lapels can be conventional double-breasted or shawl. You should have shawl or double-breasted peak style lapels even on single-breasted dinner jackets.

Step collars (that is, indented, as on an ordinary single-breasted suit) are not really correct and even the late Sir John Mills ultimately failed to make them so; although Patrick Macnee, as Steed, sometimes had these – with a velvet collar – but then he also had a frilly shirtfront; such were the times!

Subject to any directions on an invitation, either black tie or white tie may correctly be worn with a dinner jacket – and with a stiff shirt with separate wing collar or a soft shirt with a fold-down collar.

This can be confusing because a traditional alternative name for the 'dinner jacket' outfit is 'black tie'. However, there we are.

There is a nasty trap for the unwary because, although, as described, a white tie *may* be worn with a dinner jacket (as an alternative to a black tie), I emphasize that only a *white tie* may ever be worn with full fig. It has to be said that nowadays wearing a

The high life. The Duke of Windsor in a dinner jacket with shawl collar and lapels: photograph by William Lovelace/Getty Images.

white tie with a dinner jacket would be castigated by the ignorant as incorrect – and seen by the rest as eccentric.

If you disbelieve me on the options, take a look at the portrait, in **Buck's Club**, Clifford Street, Mayfair, of its founder: the redoubtable Captain Herbert Buckmaster. In this he is wearing a dinner jacket with a soft shirt and turned-down collar with a black tie and white waistcoat. He was the first husband of actress Gladys Cooper and, faced with a quantity of leftover champagne, became the inventor, in 1921, of Buck's Fizz. Besides orange juice, there is said to be also a secret ingredient known only to the barmen of the Club.

No dinner jacket is ever, outside the USA, acceptably called a 'tuxedo' – even if Mr Lobb does (and he does) make suede shoes called 'tuxedo slippers'. The word 'tuxedo' (or 'tux') is applied by Americans (and the Irish) to any short dinner jacket – and, by some, even to full fig. I have heard it said that smart East Coast Americans call a black tie dinner jacket outfit a 'dinner suit'. Along with some Germans and some Irish they also tend to wear evening dress for weddings, at any time of day. Maybe this is a reflection of the substance of the notes on very formal morning dress, above, that is to say, the fact that formal court dress has been replaced by white tie (even though ambassadors seem to be the only ones still to wear it as a substitute at court).

The use of the term 'tuxedo' came about as follows. An American tobacco millionaire, called Pierre Lorillard IV, held a party at his property, Tuxedo Park, outside New York, in October 1886. At this he wore a 'bum-freezer' type of monkey jacket (i.e. waist length, leaving the bottom uncovered) as evening wear with a black bow tie. Ever since, in the USA, such a garment has been called a tuxedo (or a 'tux').

Henry Poole first made such a jacket (along a military mess jacket pattern), in midnight blue, for wear at informal soirees for Edward, Prince of Wales, later King Edward VII, and a visitor from New York to England, in 1886 (possibly a Mr Potter), copied the style and took it back to America. Accordingly, the actual design of the garment (now normally seen as a standard short coat or 'jacket') is English and bears properly an English name, but has been popularized, elsewhere in the world, as the 'tuxedo'. Moreover, it is worthy of note that the *very first* person to wear a *midnight blue* dinner jacket was not the Duke of Windsor but his grandfather.

Have a *single* trouser stripe in silk braid. Never have turn-ups on any formal trousers – turn-ups are said to have originated with the late King Edward VII who, when Prince of Wales, turned his trousers up to avoid the mud and water in a field.

Modern dinner jacket, by Henry Poole: a wonderful example of a

CUMMERBUNDS

Cummerbunds are not naff, but a cummerbund could *become* naff if you make the mistake of wearing the cummerbund with the pleats facing *downwards – they must point upwards*. However, fancy patterned waistcoats, for morning or evening, are definitely 'naff' as they tend to undo the brilliant extinction, by Beau Brummell, of the glaring flame of foppery.

Having said this, I must emphasize that fancy Tattersall checked waistcoats are more than acceptable for daywear in the countryside. This is amply supported by the image (in Chapter 7) of the fashionable actor-manager of the early Twentieth Century, Sir Gerald du Maurier. He was the son of *Punch* magazine artist George du Maurier who also wrote the book *Trilby*, after which the Trilby hat was later named. Gerald was the father of the even more famous author, Daphne du Maurier.

TROPICAL WEIGHT WHITE OR ECRU DINNER JACKET

This could be in any of the styles described under dinner jacket, above, except that it will be made in one of the lighter materials (possibly vicuña, cashmere or mohair) and probably with a shawl collar and lapels, which could be either *faille* (corded silk) or just made of the same material as the rest of the jacket. It would be worn with the darker trousers of the dinner jacket suit.

Mohair is a strong, durable cloth made from the hair of the

Humphrey Bogart in Rick's Bar in his ecru tropical weight DJ with shawl collar and lapels: 'Of all the gin joints in all the towns in all the world, she walks into mine': photograph by SNAP/Rex Features.

Duff Cooper dressed to kill, with Susan Mary Patten. Photograph by courtesy of Artemis Cooper.

Angora goat (to be distinguished from the fluffier wool of the Angora rabbit). The hairs increase in thickness with the age of the animal – so you *don't* want a DJ made out of hair from the back of an old goat.

Last year I attended a British Council dinner in the Golden Room of the Copacabana Palace Hotel in Rio de Janeiro in one of these. Mine was the only one there and, whenever I was not actually standing with a drink in my hand, unknown people kept coming up to me, saying 'Gin and tonic' or 'Scotch'. Accordingly, beware of this item in white or ecru as it *can* make *some* people look more head barman than matinee idol.

Ecru means off-white to fawn or beige in colour, from the Old French *escru*, 'unbleached'; accordingly, one could very well have such a jacket made out of tussore (or tussar) which is unbleached raw silk produced by the larvae of the moth *Antheraea paphia*. 'Tussore' (or 'tussar') derives from the Hindi and Urdu word *tasar*. I have also seen it spelled 'tussah'. Karim Bey (the fictional head of British operations in Turkey – Station T) was wearing a lounge suit made of this when he was murdered on the train in Ian Fleming's Bond novel *From Russia With Love*.

I am not sure that actor-manager and singer Jack Buchanan ever had a tropical one although Noel Coward had one (he is wearing it in the picture on the front cover of Cole Lesley's biography of him). Humphrey Bogart wore one when he did *not* tell Sam to 'play it again' in *Casablanca*. Duff Cooper carried one off, in an ambassadorial way – but then he was British Ambassador in Paris at the time, having not long before, as Minister of Information, crossed swords with novelist P.G. Wodehouse over his wartime broadcasts on German radio (the latter always said that they were meant as satires on Nazi Germany). Duff Cooper's grand-daughter, Artemis Cooper (who has permitted me to reproduce the photograph) thinks that this jacket (possibly in silk satin) was probably made in Paris by either fashion house Dior or Balmain; because they used to give Lady Diana Cooper dresses when she was ambassadress – and because no Savile Row tailor would have been able to bring himself to produce such an article! So there we are. Let the debate begin.

EVENING SHIRTS

The starched and stiff-fronted shirt can be oval-fronted (for eating 'rosbif' in an Olde England environment, like Simpsons-in-the-Strand) or a modern (and slightly more comfortable) 'coffin-fronted' shirt which has the shape of a traditional coffin top. Simpsons-in-the-Strand was established in 1828, originally as the Grand Cigar Divan, on the site of the former, literary Kit Kat Klub. Chess matches were hosted there. Now it serves the world's best Full English Everything on big trolleys.

Soft evening shirts may have pleated fronts, as an alternative to Marcella – in which case the cuffs will be the same fabric as the rest of the shirt, sometimes a soft, sheer, cotton fabric called voile. In any case, the fronts on soft evening shirts will always be straight up and down. Marcella is a cotton or cotton and silk mix piqué fabric. Try to get the silk mix Marcella which has a gentle sheen to it, unlike the plain cotton fabric; this is very difficult to come by although I know that Budd has carried it because I have had a shirt, tie and waistcoat made from it. Unfortunately, it is virtually impossible to get it any more – and my set was made 20 years ago.

For very good versions of evening shirts of every kind, the shirt-maker Budd is hard to equal and impossible to beat, for either ready-made or bespoke, and if you take the bespoke option you will see the photographs downstairs of the late – and very great character actor – Terry-Thomas, who was a customer of one of the only (family-controlled) shirt-makers left which still cut all their goods on the premises.

There was a time when some Jermyn Street shirt-makers made even some ready-made evening shirts with formal Marcella collars, cuffs and fronts but with bodies and arms made of white material patterned with wild cartoons such as Tom and Jerry. These practices are not at all unwholesome although I confess that Jeeves would probably have observed them wryly.

A soft evening shirt, black tie and cummerbund, by Budd.

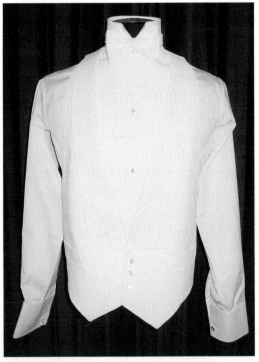

A stiff evening shirt, tie and waistcoat, by Budd.

It would be advisable to have at least three soft Marcella-fronted evening shirts with attached turned-down collars and double cuffs (also of Marcella). Additionally, you will need one or two stiff Marcella-fronted evening shirts, with separate stiff collars.

The separate collars of stiff shirts will need to be half a size larger than the shirt collar size because if you get exactly the same size as the shirt collar band there will not be enough room to get the collar right the way around – and fixing these things into place is hard enough as it is.

The shirts will have stiff single cuffs and their use will be mainly for full fig (i.e. white tie and tails). These should *not* be substituted with separate tie-on starched 'dickie fronts' – or you risk the consequences to be seen in the Marx Brothers' film *Duck Soup*.

An awful lot of rubbish (sometimes by people who should know better) has been written about evening shirts and dinner jackets. It is really very simple. One *may* wear a soft shirt with a soft turned-down collar, *or* a hard-fronted boiled shirt with a separate stiff wing collar with a dinner jacket.

Whether a stiff-fronted shirt is worn with tails (when it is *de rigueur*) or a single-breasted dinner jacket (when it is optional), it should be accompanied by either a white or dark evening waistcoat. A cummerbund is an acceptable alternative to a waistcoat with a

Wing collar and stiff shirt with a DJ and black tie: quite in order on Clark Gable who is here with his wife Carole Lombard: photograph by the John Kobal Foundation/Getty Images.

soft evening shirt and a single-breasted dinner jacket. However, a cummerbund is not appropriate with a stiff evening shirt (whether worn with tails or a dinner jacket) or with a white tie, soft shirt and dinner jacket. Neither a waistcoat nor cummerbund is necessary with a double-breasted dinner jacket, whichever type of shirt is worn.

The rot sometimes written elsewhere about evening shirts and dinner jackets derives from the fact that one simply should not wear a *soft* evening shirt with a wing collar (stiff or otherwise) as part of any kind of evening dress – unless, perhaps, when conducting an orchestra in a particularly energetic piece where asphyxiation is a real risk in the correct garment.

The evening shirt debate has got nothing to do with any inherent clash between stiff shirts with stiff wing collars and dinner jackets (or, come to that, between (the improbable) stiff turned-down collars and full fig). However, it has to be said that soft evening shirts with soft turned-down collars are, since the late Duke of Windsor adopted them, the norm for dinner jackets (also now normally worn with black tie), but there is a crucial difference between what is normal practice and what is actually correct form.

What is normal will change and *may or may not* be correct. However, what has been approved as correct form, in these respects, is never likely to change – because there are no longer detailed pronouncements from the royal court about such matters. Of course, innovations are not *necessarily* incorrect, especially those made by a sometime King of England. The modern confusion in relation to evening shirts and ties derives from the fact that soft day and evening shirts with wing collars were invented by Oxford Street and taken up by hire shops for wedding and evening hire garments.

Front studs are only really necessary with stiff shirts. With soft shirts they are unnecessary and sometimes affectation – and, usually, a very miserable one in black onyx and 'yellow metal'. However, the soft Budd evening shirt illustrated in this chapter does have interesting front studs. They may be one to three in number and be either plain gold or pearl but not diamond or something else extravagant, which might draw especial attention, such as the diamonds which 'Curricle' Coates wore. Robert 'Curricle' Coates (1772–1848) was born to a sugar plantation owner in Antigua but he later settled in Bath. He was also known as 'Diamond' Coates on account of the enormous diamond studs that he wore. A 'curricle' was a light two-wheeled chariot drawn at a canter by a pair of horses and much favoured by the man about town in the early

Nineteenth Century – including Coates. He died in a road accident.

There was a period, between the late 1940s and 1980s, when novelty, coloured (generally claret) evening ties and matching cummerbunds made an appearance with dinner jackets; this was a brief encounter with sartorial solecism exemplified by the British actor Trevor Howard in a couple of his gruff, crusty film roles. Coloured evening ties may safely be consigned to the annals of history, and tagged 'experiment: interesting but unsuccessful'.

SAFE SUMMARY

As a safe guide, for most occasions likely to be encountered today:

- White tie: where this is specified, wear the outfit described under 'Evening swallow-tail coat and trousers', silk evening half hose and evening pumps with a stiff-fronted shirt, stiff wing collar, white tie and white waistcoat.
- Black tie: where this is specified, wear the jacket and trousers described under whichever dinner jacket option is appropriate (i.e. standard-issue dark *or* 'tropical') and dark evening trousers, silk evening half hose and evening shoes or pumps, a soft-fronted shirt with soft fold-down collar and a black tie. If the dinner jacket is standard issue dark and

'Cummerbund' derives from the Urdu and Hindi word *kamarband*, itself deriving from the Persian *kamar* for 'waist' and *band* for 'band' . Several such words entered the English language as a result of the British being in India – and the item which this word denotes also entered the British wardrobe. In any event, cummerbunds were devised to be worn in hot places and so are particularly appropriate to accompany a tropical-weight dinner jacket. Bearing in mind the general light-heartedness induced by being in tropical places, why not say 'To the blazes with it all!' and wear a *very brightly coloured or even a boldly patterned one*?

single-breasted, wear a waistcoat which matches the material of the dinner jacket or a white waistcoat or a dark cummerbund. If the dinner jacket is 'tropical' ecru single-breasted, wear a cummerbund. However, if the dinner jacket (of either standard or 'tropical' kind) is double-breasted, don't worry about waistcoats or cummerbunds

EVENING TIES

Nowadays, whenever the 'media' glitterati appear at an evening gala, the men seem either to eschew ties altogether and go for the unstable rock star/Andy Warhol look in DJ and jeans or they opt for an evening tie like an ordinary 'four-in-hand' day tie which is the normal straight tie shape that is generally worn today. Surprisingly, the latter is less objectionable than it first appears. The 'four-in-hand' tie was first popularized by members of a carriage club called the 'Four in Hand Club' – and the name has nothing to do with tie knots as such. Now it is worn everyday by virtually everybody who wears a tie.

It was in fact designed by **Washington Tremlett,** in 1892, for an American called Wright, who first wore it to the opera – originally, it was intended as an unusual evening tie.

White ties are made out of the same Marcella as the shirtfronts and black ties are made out of ribbed or woven silk (sometimes called *faille*, or, of a tighter weave, *grosgrain*, which was used to make opera hats) and sometimes out of satin.

WHITE EVENING WAISTCOATS

White evening waistcoats should be in the same Marcella as the evening shirts and ties. I suggest that you should have these made, as illustrated above, single-breasted with lapels and shanked mother of pearl buttons (which should be detachable to avoid chipping in the laundry).

Remember the remark about fitting the waistcoat under the swallow-tail evening coat – make sure that whoever makes these for you has seen you in your evening coat because it is most important

that the waistcoat does not protrude from
under the sides of the coat front. Do not
be alarmed that this waistcoat will come
without a full back – just a collar and an
elastic strap. This is quite correct and
this comfortable design was probably
invented by Hawes & Curtis.

*Bespoke
Cleverley plain
Oxford evening
shoe.*

EVENING SHOES

Have these in black, patent leather or kidskin
as plain 'Oxford' lace-ups without toecaps.
Tricker's do a nice selection of ready-made lines. If
going bespoke, with such very formal clothes it can be
amusing to have an (unseen) lining in (say) postbox red.

Plain Oxford-style evening shoes (without toecaps) are normally
worn with a dinner jacket. Some people would also wear them with
full fig but this is not strictly correct, as proper evening pumps
should be worn with evening tails.

EVENING PUMPS

New & Lingwood and Tricker's do good ready-made lines in black
patent leather. Tricker's do them with or without the front bow –
those with are in the cutaway pump style with bows on the front;
those without are in the Albert style and come with bright red
linings. Most of the bespoke makers do two slight variations on the
evening pump – one with a flat bow and one with a pinched bow.
Pumps (with bows) are *de rigueur* for white tie (with trousers or
breeches) but *may* be worn with a dinner jacket.

EVENING GLOVES

Just have a pair or two of these in white or lavender kid (soft and
tight). The white variety you can get from Budd. They are very
seldom needed outside formal banquets, in royal circles or some
white tie charity balls.

A bespoke evening pump, from the Foster & Son and Henry Maxwell collection.

SMOKING SUIT

Smoking suits came about to avoid having one's normal clothes and hair reeking of the strong tobaccos which our ancestors thought were the only tobaccos worth smoking – in pipes and cigars and the fragrant (but discontinued) Sullivan Powell's Sub Rosa Oriental cigarettes; Raffles called them: 'the Royal Road to a cigar'. A smoking suit is also useful when holding dinner parties at home.

Have a smoking suit made, a dusty green silk velvet coat and trousers (possibly with a single edge of braid down the trousers), with a matching smoking hat (which Lock's should be entrusted

A fine Turnbull & Asser smoking jacket.

with) and possibly match up the slippers at W.S. Foster & Son's (proud inheritors of the famous Peal & Co. slipper tradition, which such as Douglas Fairbanks Sr swore by) or go to G.J. Cleverley and have a bespoke pair of silk velvet 'Albert' or 'Churchill' style slippers made – for the total *Wind in the Willows* Mole look. New & Lingwood also do a good to go range. On the jacket, I recommend a shawl collar and cuffs, braided edging and frogged fastenings. You would wear this with a soft evening shirt and black tie.

But I emphasize that this outfit is only for serious cigar or pipe smokers and not for anyone just chain-smoking 'light' cigarettes. You should probably also have the exclusive use of a den with a roaring log fire, if not a real smoking room. But make sure that someone else has to tend to the fire and stand or sit well away when they are doing so. If it is a real smoking room (and so no ladies present), you may curse if sparks land on you – but do remember employee rights before you get too carried away.

EVENING TOPCOAT AND HATS

It would be good to be able to run to a proper evening topcoat. Have one in black with corded silk lapel facings and basket-weave silk buttons. A bright silk lining (maybe red or purple) could also liven things up. Evening capes have, outside costume drama, gone for good and evening topcoats are on the brink and extremely rare, especially in these days when many people seem to wear day shoes and socks with evening dress. A hat for evening wear would be a black Homburg with black evening tie and a black silk topper (or opera hat) or a black Homburg with full fig.

Chapter Six

Domestic Leisure and Casual Wear

L eisure is a beautiful garment, but it will not do for constant wear. (Anon.)

INTRODUCTION

THE TROUBLE is that, today, leisure wear is, *too much*, constant wear. Of course, we all wear casual clothes and I would be a hypocrite of the first water if I denied that I did. However, we should keep some sense of place and occasion and reserve casual and leisure wear to the times and places when they are most obviously appropriate – at home and on holiday. That way, we will not find ourselves cavorting around the metropolis (at the very worst) in tracksuits and trainers, looking like lost tourists. This said, there is a range of excellent merchandise for leisure and casual wear.

DRESSING GOWNS

These could be tailored for you out of camel-coloured cashmere or vicuña for drafty castle or country-house wear and you could buy a ready-made silk or fine cotton version from a shirt-maker for cosseted London penthouse wear. There is no need to worry about complicated buttons, frogs and fittings; just go for belts. New & Lingwood and Budd and Turnbull & Asser are the tops for ready-made gowns. Noel Coward used to have

A foulard silk dressing gown in paisley pattern, by Budd.

his monogram on the breast pocket of his Sulka gowns – although, rather like Winston Churchill with his monogrammed slippers, one wonders who was likely to be in doubt as to his identity!

Foulard silk is a thin washable material of silk or silk and cotton, originally imported from India. Paisley is a place in Scotland which was one of the first places to manufacture the cloth in a replica, curled and colourful teardrop pattern (called, in Urdu – phonetically – *ambi*), first brought back, in the form of costly cashmere and silk scarves, from Kashmir to Britain, by the East India Company. The original patterns had been used in the Indian subcontinent for thousands of years. Gradually, the patterns produced in Britain developed into a flowery, westernized version of the original geometric designs and have attracted the generic name 'Paisley pattern'.

BATHROBES

I suggest that you just get a few thick white towelling robes from a good department store – or your favourite hotel (from the shop, *of course*).

PYJAMA SUITS

These are optional, except for sleeper trains (when wandering the corridor). These need to be plain but bright, or bright and boldly striped silk and incorporate large luminous mother of pearl buttons and a silken drawstring; I suggest that you get them from Budd or New & Lingwood. The original pyjama suits, of course, come from the Indian subcontinent (where they are worn all day everyday and have gigantic bloomers with a drawstring and a knee-length tunic chemise). You can get these as you pass through their countries of origin (and also in the Green Street area of East London and in Southall). They are generally sold 'free size' – which means that one size fits all – owing to the drawstring feature on the expansive bloomers and the loose fit of the tunic. These represent fabulous value for money and are tremendously comfortable garments for wearing on long-haul flights. You can complete the outfit with a gigantic shawl (the size of a thin blanket) made out of wool, cotton or cashmere – but if you hide your head inside you might be arrested on a long-haul flight these days.

HOUSE SLIPPERS

Here one could opt for the cutaway Grecian leather style or the Albert style in velvet (now called 'the Churchill' – presumably because, after noticeable declines in education few, in modern Britain, now recognize the name of the Prince Consort to Queen Victoria). Consider having also a pair of house slippers in turkey red leather (they used to be available ready-made from several firms; now (sadly) they are generally available only as bespoke or by special order) or even genuine (and cheaper) ornately embroidered oriental leather slippers (worn without socks) from the many clothing stores in Green Street, East London, or in Southall, West London. I noticed that **Berk** are doing a black velvet number with golden moons and stars embroidered on them. Such firms as G.J. Cleverley, W.S. Foster & Son and New & Lingwood do good ready-made plain velvet ones, but it is cotton (rather than silk) velvet. If

Foster & Son bespoke slippers and motifs.

you want silk velvet that sparkles as though bejewelled you will have to supply it yourself and pay the price for bespoke or special order. I have tried velvet slippers recently but I wear my footwear too hard to justify replacing them – within a few weeks, they were thoroughly beaten up. My environment is also sandy and dusty from the beach and garden, which means that they end up needing a brush twice a day.

BATH SLIPPERS

For these cashmere felt is best and most shoe-makers and the shops in the Arcades have these ready-made. Lobb's also do them bespoke – if you have just over £500 sloshing around without a home.

CASUAL SHIRTS

It would be an idea to have, say, half a dozen 'polo shirts' for sitting by the pool. **Thomas Pink** does a very good line – with drawn-in short-sleeve ends, effective to disguise spindly arms. (The phrase *in the pink*, denoting happiness, derives from the satisfaction which customers felt when they wore hunt coats made by an Eighteenth-Century tailor called Thomas Pink.) Also useful are a few short-sleeved Hawaiian shirts with bright, floral patterns for places where it is 30 degrees by 9.30 am – and just too hot to wear much at all. You could have these made up at Budd in West Indian Sea Island cotton. A breast pocket on casual shirts is acceptable and indeed sensible, because it provides storage space when it is not likely to be readily available elsewhere. It might even be an idea to have a large pocket with a flap and button, for added security. One would generally avoid pockets on shirts – especially on formal shirts.

JUMPERS

There are plenty of suppliers of jumpers in and around the Arcades. You can choose from cashmere, merino, lambs' wool and West Indian Sea Island cotton. High West Indian Sea Island cotton polo necks are good for golf or chillier tropical evenings. There is nothing wrong with Marks & Spencer again now either. **N. Peal,** of the Burlington Arcade, and **John Smedley** (several general outlets) are the main players here. Fair Isle jumpers are also ideal for golf in Scotland; tank tops in this were popularized – especially for golf – by the Duke of Windsor when Prince of Wales. The woollens comprise stranded colour work knitting, in patterns with palettes limited to around five colours for each item.

There are also ranges of shorter, informal coats available from suppliers such as Alfred Dunhill.

DENIM JEANS

The name derives from 'de Nimes' in France. Levi Strauss is too well known to need much introduction here. However, there is now (as a sign of the times, What! What!) a bespoke jeans maker in Savile Row, **Evisu** (a Japanese clothes designer), and Huntsman confesses that it recently experimented with making bespoke jeans but has now given up on the exercise. The actress Katharine Hepburn, no doubt inspired by Spencer Tracy's patronage of them, once ordered such things from them. I am told that jeans are sometimes now worn with sports training shoes of various kinds – and there we are. A pair of Cleverley or Foster & Son's loafers might be a better idea. If you want some smart American shirting to go with your jeans and trainers, **Brooks Bros** (most famous for their signature button-down collars) have opened a shop in Regent Street, but, as we know, from Chapter 1, bespoke shirt-makers can do any style that you wish.

A Cleverley loafer.

SUEDE CASUAL SHOES

Berluti's 'Dandy' style is attractive; and there is also Tricker's tasselled 'loafer' style ('loafer' derives from the Urdu word for 'layabout'). Lobb's have a very large catalogue of smart casual bespoke shoe designs, ranging from tuxedo slippers to Norwegian loafers, which you can have made up in any material you wish.

Tennis shoes

One would opt for Dunlop plimsolls, out of nostalgia, obviously, unless you are a star of British tennis when the order of the day would seem to be hobnail boots, with extra ironwork, from your local man. However, the plimsolls would seem to meet the case if you are just one of next year's hopeful spectators on 'Henman Hill'; 'Murray Mount' or 'Bumbler's Bump'. The fore-runners of modern plimsolls were developed by the Liverpool Rubber Company in the 1830s. The company became Dunlop (famous now mainly for motorcar tyres). Plimsolls were *de rigueur* for gym classes around the world until the onset (and peculiar popularity) of sweat-trapping 'training shoes'. Plimsolls probably got their modern name from the resemblance of the rubber banding, connecting the uppers and soles, to the Plimsoll load lines which were introduced on ships in 1876, as a result of the efforts of politician Samuel Plimsoll to save lives at sea.

Chapter Seven

Country and Sporting Dress

I covet not a wider range
Than these dear manors give;
I take my pleasures without change,
And as I lived I live.

I leave my neighbours to their thought;
My choice it is, and pride,
On my own lands to find my sport,
In my own fields to ride.
(From 'The Old Squire', by Wilfred Scawen Blunt)

INTRODUCTION

Country life in the United Kingdom – especially in England – is under threat: from various, obvious, urban activists and, not least, from the policies of central and local government, with their unspeakable programmes for the wholesale demolition of some of our old market towns (and the consequential loss of the communities in them) and their replacement (under the guise of 'regional development') by the erection of swathes of prefabricated, multi-storey, concrete and plasterboard boxes across the landscape; criss-crossed with motorways. Add to all of that, the destructive force of the European Union's agricultural policies (paying farmers not to use land, under the 'set aside' provisions), the fact that English Heritage's starting place for listing applications appears to be not to list (especially in relation to buildings erected after 1914), and it probably won't be long before the whole land is a checker-board of shoddy housing, tarmac and empty retail space; all with a life expectancy of about twenty-five years (cynically calculated according to the length of the mortgage terms which will pay for them). However, it is still just about possible to enjoy country sports and so this chapter is about how to appear when you attend some of the various activities.

COUNTRY SHIRTS

I suggest that you add to the total of your day shirts two or three white or cream hunting shirts and hunting stocks. **Swaine Adeney Brigg** are the chaps for ready-made hunting shirts. John Ross was established as a whip-maker in Piccadilly in 1750. James Swaine bought him out in 1798 and royal warrants followed a burgeoning business. They moved to larger premises and won medals at the Great Exhibition in 1851 and at the Paris Exhibition in 1900. Meanwhile, Thomas Brigg & Sons had been umbrella and stick makers in St James's Street since 1836 and secured the first royal warrant as suppliers of umbrellas (to Queen Victoria) in 1893. As a result of the exigencies and losses of the Second World War, the firms merged in 1943.

You should also have some Tattersall checked viyella (brushed cotton) shirts for general weekend country wear from Cording's, who were established on the Strand side of Temple Bar in 1839 and moved to 19 Piccadilly in 1871. Famed for waterproofs, Newmarket field boots and Tattersall checked shirts and waistcoats, they locked horns with Burberry in a High Court case in 1909, over the use of the phrase 'slip-on' (in relation to waterproofs). Cording's won. More recently, the company was subject to a management buy-out with the support of guitarist Eric Clapton.

CAVALRY TWILL TROUSERS

Have these, which comprise a strong worsted twill in a herringbone pattern, once favoured by cavalry regiments, in ducal, light colours; for slouching at home or for the Alan Whicker look – but only he may sport them with a blazer or reefer jacket. If you are not Alan Whicker (and despite an article by style guru and historian, Nick

Foulkes, in *Country Life*, quoting Evelyn Waugh about the undesirability of tweed coats with 'flannels'), try a tweed coat instead. In fact, if I may say so, even if you are Alan Whicker (*pace, pace*), try a tweed coat instead. Have these trews tailored or go to Cording's or Hackett.

CORDUROY TROUSERS

These are made from a corded cotton velvet fabric, probably first manufactured in Manchester and not (despite the obvious derivation of the name from corde du roi – king's cloth) in France. They are for maintaining the same image as that projected by cavalry twill trousers, above – but these are more Colonel Blimp than Alan Whicker. Oliver Brown, **Harvie & Hudson** (still a family firm and famous for the bold stripes of their shirts) and Hackett do good lines in many colours; I am not too sure about *all* the colours but at least the variety is there. There is no need to tailor these and they are ideal with Argyle socks (undoubtedly of Scottish origin, they are socks with diamond patterns; one theory is that they derive from foot coverings cut on the bias, i.e. diagonally, out of tartan plaids). They are also ideal for golf. Wear also a good thick merino wool jumper for taking the 1931 8 litre Bentley or the 1939 4.75 litre Derby Bentley ('The silent sportscar') down for a tyre change.

GOLFING SHOES

Tricker's do a good 'to go' range but, if you are a budding Arnold Palmer or Tiger Woods, I suppose that you will have to bespeak and so maybe you will have G.J. Cleverley,

W.S. Foster & Son's, Henry Maxwell's or Poulsen Skone do the job
– or you will saunter down to Lobb's. They will also do your ski
boots, if you are so inclined – but have plenty of cash with you.
Golfing shoes are traditionally in a full brogue style, with a fringed
outer tongue to keep the water off the laces and have under-studs to
grip the turf.

CARDIGANS

These come in cashmere, merino, lambs' wool, alpaca – or whatever
– in Granny's cable stitch and in any colour as long as it's oxblood
red, sparrow brown or bottle green. Strictly for the Uncle Harry type
(young or old) – these are otherwise generally discommended unless
you are so old that you can no longer physically go for the jumper
option. However, **N. Peal** (established in the Burlington Arcade in
1936 to market cashmere woollens – they buy the wool in Mongolia
and China and work it in Scotland) and the **Berk** do stock these.

SHOOTING SUIT

This should comprise a fairly standard pattern
tweed coat and knickerbockers (plus twos); maybe
in a restrained checked pattern;
combining camouflage colours of
greens, blues, purples, browns and rust.
Have leather shoulder patches and
maybe other trimmings – together with
horn buttons. Shoulder vents give
room to swing your arms around. It is

Shooting jacket, by Norton &
Sons, showing shoulder patch,
patch pockets and lapel tab
(ghillie collar) for doing the front
up completely if the going gets
rough.

Bespoke tweed shooting breeches, by Norton & Sons.

clear also from the illustrations that Norton & Sons would be difficult to beat in this area. Worn self-consciously (by the wrong person), this item *could* shout 'City Slicker' when worn off one's own land – at, say, commercially organized shoots – so remember to turn your 'BlackBerry' off.

There is, of course, a choice between plus fours or plus twos or knee breeches. Beware of vulgar loud garters and remember Emma Willis for shooting stockings (covered in Chapter 1). Plus fours would be more usual for golf and might get too wet shooting. With plus twos or knee breeches, there is the opportunity to wear leather greaves around the shins (which are basically buckled or buttoned leather leggings, similar to medieval leg armour, without a galosh top to fix over the shoes) if not high gaiters (which are long canvas spats with galosh tops). You would have to go bespoke on both of these items today; and any of the good bespoke boot-makers could (with indulgently raised eyebrows) oblige. Norton & Sons and Bernard Weatherill are especially noted for bespoke country and sporting clothes.

GENERAL SPORTING BREECHES

Have a pair in plain green moleskin for the rougher days with rubber wellies or for fishing in waders. Cording's do these breeches and they make quite the Robin Hood look.

HUNTING COAT AND WAISTCOAT

Have a black Melton cloth coat. If you go for the (shorter) hacking jacket style of coat, you will need buff buckskin breeches and butcher boots (i.e. high riding boots without contrasting 'tops'). If you adopt the frock hunting coat approach, you should have top boots (with mahogany or champagne tops – as illustrated) and white buckskin breeches. In both cases, high hunt spurs should be worn (without rowels or the blunt spinning, pronged wheels, attached to military spurs). The formal hunting shirt and stock are appropriate.

The Ratcatcher is informal wear worn for autumnal cub hunting and comprises tweed hacking jacket, buff breeches, viyella shirt and Tattersall checked waistcoat with a suitable woollen tie bearing a hunting motif. Butcher boots (sometimes canvas Newmarket boots) are worn. A hacking jacket is a specialized item and is longer and fuller than a standard 'sports' jacket.

In any event, no one may wear hunting scarlet (or 'pink') – or any other particular hunt colours – or hunt buttons, unless the right to do so has been awarded by the Master of the Hunt. Some hold that the colour hunting scarlet is a hangover from the fact that scarlet is the predominant colour of Royal Livery and hunting rights derive

VANITY FAIR Supplement.

Heurschel-Colourtype, London.

Sir Gerald du Maurier in a Tattersall checked waistcoat.

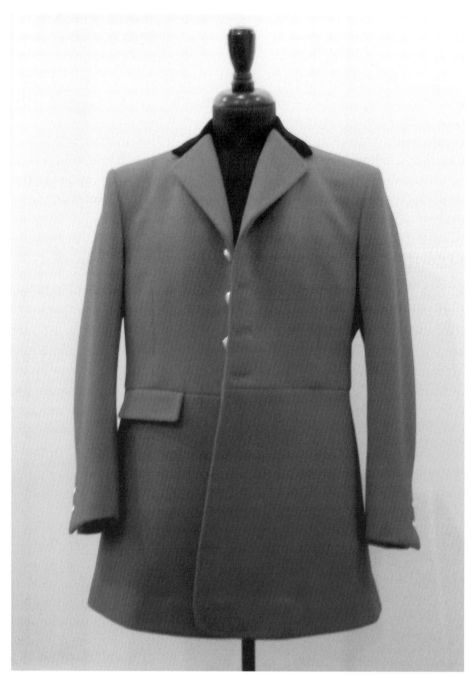

A recent scarlet frock hunting coat, by Norton & Sons.

from the Crown. With formal hunt colours, a hard velvet hunt cap may be worn as an alternative to a topper. These are supplied by Lock's and a firm, away down in Dulwich, called **Patey's**.

Again, Norton & Sons would be impossible to beat for the clothing. Dege (& Skinner) also specialize in hunt coats. The waistcoat with hunt dress is often either plain canary yellow, or else cream with a discreet ('Tattersall') check – this can be bought at Cording's, who originally adapted the patterns on horse blankets at Newmarket to waistcoats and shirting. You can, of course, take the bespoke option. When mounted keep all your coat buttons done up.

HUNTING BREECHES

Go to Swaine Adeney or Cording's for ready-made ones or to Bernard Weatherill for bespoke. As mentioned already, they say that they believe (and they are unchallenged) that they are the last actually to make bespoke riding breeches; however, if one asked Norton & Sons they would not fail you; the cutter would be different but they would use the same tailor to make them up. Connock & Lockie have a splendid antique pair, in a military pattern, on a stand in their shop and they undoubtedly have the knowledge and expertise to replicate them and variations on a theme.

REEFER JACKET/BLAZER

'Blazer' was the term originally applied to the red jackets of members of the Lady Margaret Hall Boat Club (which, presumably, blazed); it was also applied to the blue serge uniform jackets which the Captain of HMS *Blazer* had made for his ratings when the ship was inspected by Queen Victoria. I suggest having this made in double-breasted navy blue serge, with gilt shank buttons of your choice (probably Nelson buttons – gilt buttons bearing the representation of an anchor at an angle and a scroll), sloping pockets (including ticket pocket), preferably *with no flaps on the pockets*. A blazer sometimes has patch pockets but the reefer jacket standard coat pockets are rather smarter for general use. Have either standard double-breasted with two 'show' buttons at the top or you could have all three to do up. If you have the show buttons, just do up the top button, which is meant to do up. If you have three to do up, do them all up, although when sitting you will need to undo (at least) the lower two. Vents (for double-breasted) may be two or none at all. A reefer jacket or a blazer is worn with one of the following two items and not with grey flannels.

WHITE DUCKS

Have half a dozen pairs of self-supporting trousers: either the real thing, in unbleached linen and bespoke, or you should know that Hackett and Oliver Brown do good linen

A bespoke blazer, by Norton & Sons.

summer trousers (in various colours); albeit with rather skimped two darts at the waistband, rather than four. When you have these you might experiment by emulating the seafaring style of King George V (as made up for him by Davies & Son) and have the trouser creases put side to side instead of fore and aft. Plainly, this sort of clothing (in proper unbleached duck) and indeed the blazer are very much in the line of bespoke touring clothing for which Norton & Sons are famed.

WHITE FLANNELS

These would be the same as the immediately preceding entry, except made in flannel, which is a brushed woollen fabric and is, in fact, the material used for George V's seafaring wear, mentioned above.

CO-RESPONDENT SHOES

So called because they were the sort of thing that a co-respondent to a divorce petition would have worn in the days of adultery suits with 'tecs in stained fawn macs and battered hats and evidence gleaned from the edgy, lubricious servants of seedy, seaside hotels. For a similar reason, brown suede shoes are often known as 'brothel creepers'. I am seriously considering a pair of co-respondent shoes in post-box red leather and white buckskin; to be worn with a red and white Hawaiian shirt and white ducks. Most ready-made co-respondent shoes are made with white leather rather than buckskin (or 'nubuck') and leather is, strictly, just *not* correct. The styles normally seen are the Oxford or the half brogue or the full brogue (known in other places as the 'wing-tip'). The full brogue is the most common ready-made version (in black or brown and white). The simple Oxford toecap style is, to my mind, much smarter.

TWEED COUNTRY TOP COAT

Have this in single-breasted rich orange snuff-coloured Harris Tweed herringbone maybe with Raglan sleeves. I always think that tweed coats should be single-breasted: double-breasted is to my mind (and it is just an opinion) strictly metropolitan.

WAXED COAT

Very obviously this means thorn-proof Barbour; standard and everywhere – to keep the spray-on mud off the other clothes on the way home to Fulham, after a Sunday on Cla'ham Common. I am not sure that Brummell would have had one of these – but then nor did he live in Fulham or wallow in (canned or any) mud. I prefer the shorter types, rather than the long jobs which make the wearer look like one of the gentlemen in the verse about smugglers which goes 'Brandy for the parson; 'baccy for the Clerk . . .

Watch the wall, my darling, as the gentlemen go by.' The usual one is the short 'Beaufort' style.

LODEN CAPE

Kettner's do the standard dark green version – and they are great for country walks (quite the Rider Haggard look) – but I have been warned off saying that these may be worn for shooting parties in the United Kingdom and Eire – and the chap who has warned me off is a damned fine shot.

RUBBER WELLINGTON BOOTS

As mentioned under the bespoke section of town shoes, Hoby the Great made the Iron Duke's original campaign boots which have been adapted (even by the French, against whom they were so effective) into state of the art, practical, modern, rubber, field or gum boots. There are (for the moment anyway) even leather-lined, zip-up **Hunter** 'Crown' leather wellies: top of the range; for home on the range – or snug in the Range Rover. Cording's do them. Hunter wellies also come in cheaper versions, including just plain rubber. For another type at the top of the range there is **Le Chameau**

Chasseur Prestige leather-lined, zip-up natural rubber ground hunting boots. You can get these by mail order.

COUNTRY SHOES

For brown heavy-weight shoes, definitely consider Tricker's heavy grain calf (or crup – horse leather) ready-made full brogues – but I would not go for the great rounded clodhoppers (like something out of Hans Christian Andersen), for which they are curiously famous. I know of someone who failed to catch a burglar he alarmed on returning to his house because he had gone clodhopper for the day. However, if you are going bespoke, Henry Maxwell, W.S. Foster & Son and G.J. Cleverley all have a range of styles. You will find that these shoes need to be treated with dubbin (a preparation of wax, oil and tallow) to keep the water out when out in the field, walking or shooting. Obviously if you go into high grass and deep coverts you will need to move into wellies or the Newmarket field boots.

RIDING BOOTS (BUTCHER BOOTS AND CHAMPAGNE OR MAHOGANY TOP BOOTS)

Champagne coloured tops make a change from the more usual mahogany colour. You will really have to go bespoke on these in waxed calf (i.e. suede side up) which, as already mentioned, you will have to have rubbed with a deer bone and blacking to polish. Henry Maxwell, Foster & Son and

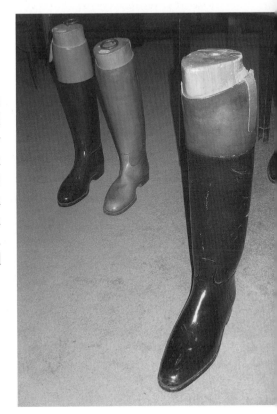

Mahogany top boot, tan coloured butcher boot and a champagne top boot all in the Foster & Son and Henry Maxwell collection.

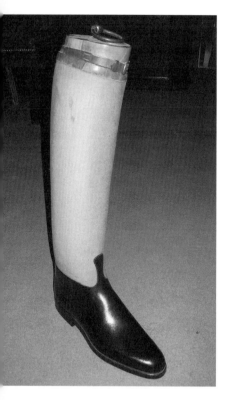

John Lobb's are the places. You will also need large, expensive trees for the whole boot and a boot jack to get them on and off.

NEWMARKET FIELD BOOTS

These are made of leather and canvas and are indispensable for shooting on very wet days or for hacking. Cording's are famous for their ready-made versions of these boots and, for many years, they kept one, harmlessly submerged in a tank of water, in the window. However, Henry Maxwell and Foster & Son still make these bespoke for the fastidious.

Canvas and leather bespoke Newmarket boot in the Foster & Son and Henry Maxwell collection.

Chapter Eight

Hats

Where did you get that hat,
Where did you get that tile,
And isn't it a nobby one,
And what a proper style.
I should like to have one just the same as that;
Where'er I go they shout, Helloa,
Where did you get that hat.

HATS: GENERAL NOTE AND GUIDANCE AND SOME VIEWS

HATS ARE not now generally fashionable for English men or for English women and long gone is the time when the rule applied that soft felt hats were unacceptable wear for a man before the London Summer Season had finished. This season used to extend from Queen Charlotte's Ball in May (begun by George III in 1780 to raise money for charity), through to the racing at Goodwood at the beginning of August. It is thought that the phenomenon of 'the season' began with the restoration of Charles II in 1660. The formal presentation of debutantes at court was officially abolished by the Queen in 1958 (by when, in any event, debutantes were presented to a large white cake, to which they made a curtsey), and the season started a long decline. Vestiges remain: the Royal Academy Summer Exhibition, Royal Ascot, the Summer Berkeley Dress Show, Henley Royal Regatta, the Chelsea Flower Show, Wimbledon Fortnight, Lord's, Cowes Week and 'Glorious' Goodwood (described by Edward VII as 'a garden party with racing tacked on').

A hundred years ago, only formal hats (i.e. top hats and cokes – otherwise known as 'bowlers') were the order of the day in town during the season. R. Brimley Johnson's *Manners Makyth Man* records that in the Eighteenth Century a man would have risked being spat upon for not wearing a hat in the street. Maybe it's a moot point whether the fact that this no longer happens is the mark of lost standards. Often people, such as the poet William Cowper, even wore linen caps, smoking hats and nightcaps indoors.

My grandparents always wore hats (even to go into the garden) and my father (and I) do so still. Forty years ago, women wore a hat most of the time – and certainly to church and to any remotely 'arranged' function. Sometimes, they wore headscarves (for which Hermes became famous) instead. But one or other was mandatory; as a matter of what jurisprudential philosophers would call positive morality or custom: full of social but of no legal force. The rot set in with JFK ('hatless Jack', President Kennedy) who often went without a hat. A couple of years ago, I heard a woman told by a court usher *to take her hat off* in court! The sense of loss which this occasioned is beyond description because it was an official demonstration that the barbarians are through the gates and even officialdom is infected with the consequential profound ignorance. We must also recall, with Charles Baudelaire, that 'Dandyism is the last gleam of heroism in times of decadence.'

There are times, such as Royal Ascot, weddings and so forth when a man's hat is ceremonially worn (or carried). When court dress still comprised tail coat, breeches, sword and court shoes with steel buckles, a *chapeau bras* was carried but, in fact, was actually *incapable of being worn*: it just did not have a head hole big enough. Lock & Co. sold them as 'arm hats' which, of course, is just a straight translation from the French.

ADMIRAL LORD NELSON'S HATS

Lock's most famous and priceless real hats are national treasures. They are the bicorne (two-cornered) beaver felt cocked hats which belonged to Admiral Lord Nelson (his hats varied in size between size 7 full and size 7 1/8 full). When one loses or gains weight it is often most apparent in the fitting of clothes around one's waist line – but it will also change the fit of rings on the fingers and hats on the head! Lock & Co.'s company archives include the customer head sizes and, since the introduction of the *conformateur* in the 1850s, also the head shapes in the cardboard 'conforms', which provide details of customers' head shapes and sizes.

The *conformateur* is a device which looks as though it has ascended from the Stygian depths to inflict some cruel and unusual punishment but is, in fact, a skeleton hat with moveable parts to frame the head, according to its phrenology – or its peculiar lumps and bumps. It then reproduces the shape on a small piece of card, which is used to mould any hard-shelled hat, over heat, to the purchaser's exact dimensions. Janet Taylor of Lock & Co. explained to me that the resulting conform cards show that the British head shape has, on average, increased by at least three-eighths of an inch in circumference every half century. These conform cards are a phrenologist's field day and something of a trap for those who adamantly refuse to acknowledge that time and weight can change their head size. It would appear that, in Lord Nelson's case, his continuing ill health led to a loss in weight and a reduction of his hat size from 7 1/8 full to 7 full by 1805.

I have been told, by Dr Kenneth Cliff (family member and part-

Inside Nelson's hat in Westminster Abbey is the maker's name and a stamp showing that Hat Tax had been paid. Hat Tax was a duty levied, between 1784–1811, on the sale of hats. The amount of tax increased with the cost of the hat. It was enforced by a system of fines for non-payment, but the death penalty applied for forgery of the revenue stamps. Other similar taxes were Window Tax (1697–1851) – causing some people to block up unnecessary windows, with the results still to be seen in old buildings; Glove Tax (1785–94) and Hair Powder Tax (1786–1869) from the times when people wore powdered wigs.

time archivist of James Lock & Co.), that Lord Nelson ordered two hats from them in 1805 and it is likely that both of these (with the special eyeshade, described below) were with him on his last voyage to Trafalgar. There is a Lock & Co. hat on his wax effigy in Westminster Abbey (despite his prediction before the Battle of the Nile, 'Before this time tomorrow, I shall have gained a Peerage or Westminster Abbey', he was actually buried, like the Duke of Wellington, in St Paul's Cathedral).

This hat is fitted with a green eyeshade over the central part of the hat (*not an eye patch*) *to shield his remaining good eye, which was his left eye.* His right eye had been badly injured by a bursting shell and sand bags

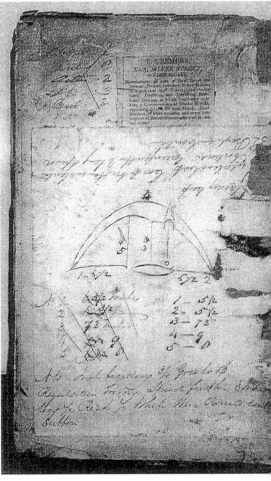

The design, made by James Lock II and his foreman, of the hat, with eyeshade.

during the siege of Calvi. He lost virtually all the sight in his right eye and had been advised to shield his eyes from the light, especially since he suffered from other eye conditions as he got older. Lord Nelson (also using his Sicilian title, Duke of Bronte) had first visited Lock's on Tuesday 11 November 1800. The first eyeshade attachment was designed between Lord Nelson and James Lock II and his foreman on 11 February 1803 and the agreed price (including cockade) was two guineas. Lock's still have the ledger containing the drawing of the hat with attached eyeshade.

Apart from the hat, the rest of his (blood-stained) undress Trafalgar uniform (made by 'Old Mel' Meredith, naval tailor, in Portsmouth) is in the National Maritime Museum, except his shoes and outer shirt which were lost – the shoes at the battle scene and the outer shirt after it was removed from his body when it was taken from the cask of spirits which brought his body home. The blood still visible on his uniform is probably not just his because the deck would have been awash with blood.

Although he wore all his British decorations during the battle (in accordance with naval regulations and *not*, as sometimes suggested, out of personal vanity), he did not wear his diamond aigrette, the Plume of Triumph, in his hat. He just wore a plain cockade, as supplied by Lock & Co., and it has been pointed out to me, by Dr Kenneth Cliff, that paintings of him at Trafalgar in a full-dress naval hat, with gold lace, are inaccurate. Nelson's cockade was basically a plain black ribbon rosette. Bishops wore similar (but smaller) rosettes on the hatbands of their black silk toppers into the Twentieth Century and examples of these are in Lock's shop. These adornments might account for the old expression: 'fussier than a Bishop's hat'. One has in mind the press photograph of the hatted and gaitered Archbishop of Canterbury, Cosmo Gordon Lang, as he strode out of 10 Downing Street at the height of the Abdication crisis in 1936.

The National Maritime Museum has the hat which Lord Nelson wore during the Battle of Copenhagen on 2 April 1801, when he famously put the telescope to his blind right eye and disobeyed Admiral Sir Hyde Parker's signal to discontinue the action. There were *at least* two Lock hats at

A painting, by Ken Hutchinson, of Lord Nelson's hat with eyeshade.

> The Plume of Triumph (or *chelengk*) had been the gift of Selim III, Ottoman Sultan, for Lord Nelson's part in the Battle of the Nile on 1 August 1798, preserving his empire from Napoleonic expansionism. This important decoration (designed as a turban decoration for valour) included 13 plumes encrusted with Brazilian diamonds, which fanned out on plates and vibrated with movement. A clockwork device made the central jewel rotate and, in catching the light, sparkle even more. Each plume represented a French ship taken in the battle. Although, in his lifetime, Lord Nelson generally stored it in the bank, it was stolen from a public display in a planned raid on the National Maritime Museum by some utter tyke(s) in 1951.

the Battle of Copenhagen because Admiral Sir Hyde Parker himself was also a Lock customer.

Lord Nelson wore his hats athwart, like Bonaparte, rather than fore and aft, like the Duke of Wellington (another Lock customer). The last Lock hat with eyeshade was delivered to Lord Nelson on 10 September 1805 (before the Battle of Trafalgar on 21 October 1805). It cost him two pounds six shillings – four shillings more than the first one. He paid his account, dating from 1803, in the sum of eleven pounds and nineteen shillings and sixpence, on Friday 13 September 1805. Then he went home to Lady Hamilton and their daughter Horatia at Merton before he sailed from Portsmouth on HMS *Victory* and out into legend.

SOME PRACTICAL CONSIDERATIONS

Sometimes, hats are useful to keep warm or dry. A lot of heat is lost through an unprotected head. Also, sun hats are becoming essential in parts of the world, owing to 'global warming' and, in some states in Australia, pupils are turned away from schools unless they pitch up with a 'titfer' (Cockney rhyming slang – 'tit-for-tat = hat').

Hat etiquette

In any event, whenever a hat is worn by a man, he *must* observe a few fundamental rules of etiquette; even though, according to Captain Jesse, Brummell never removed his hat ceremonially outside (for fear of disarranging his coiffure) but instead used to extend his arm, in a kind of Roman salute, to acquaintances. On the other hand, French kings under the *ancien régime* developed a whole series of different acknowledgements of their acquaintance with their headgear, according to their particular rank.

There used to be a tradition at Eton, known as 'capping' – when boys would salute the Beaks in the street by pointing a finger at their heads, as an abbreviated doffing of the hat (like a naval or military salute); this would be reciprocated by the Beaks. Recently, despite government drives for the promotion of what it is pleased to call 'respect', this tradition has died out: I suppose that it takes too much time and effort and shows too much *deference* – so, like many similar customs, it is doomed in modern Britain. In fairness, soon after having written the above, I was cheered to note that many of the golfers in the British Open are still doffing their caps to the crowd at the end of their rounds (described by the commentator Peter Aliss as 'an old world custom – nothing wrong with that' – quite so).

Except for smoking hats, hats should not nowadays be worn inside a domestic dwelling (*pace* the late Jack Buchanan who wore his Herbie Johnson pearl-grey trilby at home; presumably on the basis of the advertising slogan that 'A man with a **Herbert Johnson** hat is a man apart').

Especially don't wear a hat in someone else's home; nor in a lift in any building if a lady or elderly person is present. They may be worn in the public bar of a tavern – but one should not be there in the first place. They may be worn inside large shops but not small ones (especially when a female is serving); they used to be worn in the clubs of St James's, but are no longer; they are, of course, worn at railway stations, on trains, horses, elephants and bicycles, in motor cars and at racecourses. They should never be worn in restaurants

Herbert Johnson had been encouraged to start up as a hatter in partnership with John Glazier in 1889 (at 45 New Bond Street) by King Edward VII (as Prince of Wales) after Johnson one day rescued the prince's hat when it blew off in the park. Some of those who took up Herbert Johnson included Nikolay Aleksandrovich Romanov, last Emperor and Autocrat of all the Russias (Czar Nicholas II), who was forced to abdicate in the first Russian revolution of 1917, caused largely by what the historian A.L. Rowse always called the 'First German War', started by another Johnson customer, Prinz Friedrich Wilhelm Albert Viktor Hohenzollern, the last German Emperor and King of Prussia (Kaiser Wilhelm II), who was also forced to abdicate, for much the same reason as his cousin. It's a pity that these chaps didn't share King Edward VII's political nous – as well as his taste in hats.

or at a table anywhere except al fresco. Wearers of baseball caps in restaurants should be seized by four waiters (one at each limb), vigorously given the bumps and, regardless of weather conditions, swung out into the street.

Hats must be removed when entering a church or other place of Christian worship (even if one is merely a tourist), at a service by a war memorial, for a passing hearse and at a Christian graveside; just as they should be clamped securely on when visiting a synagogue, a Sikh temple or a mosque. Hats should be politely doffed to ladies and elderly persons (when passing or departing); some hold that, when greeting and stopping to speak to a lady or the elderly, one should remove one's headgear altogether. When passing or departing from male acquaintances, one should just touch or point at the brim or peak (or, as with a jinnah cap, just point at the head). Men used to lift their hats when passing the Cenotaph and when the National Anthem was played – and it used to be played rather a lot. It was played at the end of a cinema performance and at the end of the day's broadcasting by the BBC.

Then, of course, there is The Big Black Car. I recall once walking up the east side of St James's Square when I saw a flash of deep black metal gliding around the corner from the north: a Rolls Royce Phantom VI with no number plates. Just in time, I turned and stopped and raised my hat high into the air, as the Duke of Edinburgh appreciatively pushed out his left arm and raised his hand.

Obviously, soft hats are removed by the crown, hard hats by the brim and caps by the peak. Astrakhan jinnah forage caps are pulled off from the front of the crown. I do not deal expressly with the naval, military and diplomatic customs since each of these is *sui generis* and knowledge of the correct drill is part of the training. I am not sure whether any governors-general (vice-regal delegates who perform the functions of the Crown in Commonwealth countries, which retain the Crown of the United Kingdom as the head of state) still wear full fig – including bicorne cocked hat and swan plumes. Cabinet ministers long since ceased routinely to wear uniforms – often military or as Privy Counsellors.

THE NECESSARY HATS TO HAVE

Black silk top hat (preferably marked inside 'extra quality')

This is thought to have been invented by a Mr John Hetherington and first worn by him in public in February 1797 when it literally caused a riot and he was bound over in the then enormous sum of £500 to keep the peace. Originally, they were made of lustrous beaver fur felt. The last people to wear the later silk version daily were stockjobbers but they ceased the practice in 1986. They had maintained the tradition of the top hat for so long in order to be easily identifiable, for the purpose of effecting quick transactions. Moreover, the top hat remained in daily procedural use in the House of Commons until 1998, when it was abolished under a programme of modernization. So, in a real sense, a version of this hat was in everyday fashion for an unbroken period of around two centuries.

In their day, Lock's customers included Beau Brummell and the other Regency dandies, bucks and beaux: such as the 2nd Earl of

Regency Bond Street Loungers.

Sefton, the 5th Duke of Devonshire, 'Poodle' Byng (The Hon Frederick Gerald Byng whose habit it was to parade around fashionable areas with a curly French poodle), Lord Manners and the 6th Duke of Beaufort; all featured in the 1820 illustration *The Well Known Bond Street Loungers*. Each prided himself on the unique fit and style of his top hat, choosing a shape to complement his silhouette.

Now the item is either proudly inherited, reconditioned or purchased, refurbished, from Lock's or Herbert Johnson or Patey's – or discovered in a junk shop and then ordered to be reconditioned by them. There are also traders who deal exclusively in this item – such as **Ascot Top Hats** and **Hetherington Hats**. The last factory to make the napped silk velvet ('hatter's plush') which famously went into them was owned by a pair of brothers in Lyons but they fell out

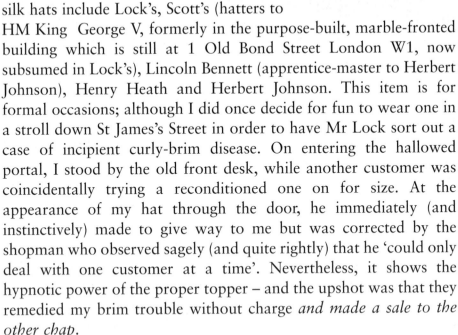

Refurbished silk top hat, of a type available from Lock & Co.

and smashed up the looms (bloody fools!). Now, ironically, the best modern black top hats are produced once again using felt containing lustrous beaver or rabbit fur.

Famous blasts from the past for silk hats include Lock's, Scott's (hatters to HM King George V, formerly in the purpose-built, marble-fronted building which is still at 1 Old Bond Street London W1, now subsumed in Lock's), Lincoln Bennett (apprentice-master to Herbert Johnson), Henry Heath and Herbert Johnson. This item is for formal occasions; although I did once decide for fun to wear one in a stroll down St James's Street in order to have Mr Lock sort out a case of incipient curly-brim disease. On entering the hallowed portal, I stood by the old front desk, while another customer was coincidentally trying a reconditioned one on for size. At the appearance of my hat through the door, he immediately (and instinctively) made to give way to me but was corrected by the shopman who observed sagely (and quite rightly) that he 'could only deal with one customer at a time'. Nevertheless, it shows the hypnotic power of the proper topper – and the upshot was that they remedied my brim trouble without charge *and made a sale to the other chap.*

The inside hatband should be a broad swathe of white leather, bearing one's initials in gold leaf.

A cloth-lined collapsible opera hat

Otherwise known as a *chapeau claque* or, in France – after its ingenious inventor – as a Gibus, this would seem an extravagance but Lincoln Bennett and Walter Barnard (formerly of Jermyn Street) did nice ones *Open opera hat* which can sometimes be had second-hand from the sources mentioned above. Also, an exquisite, eminently stylish opera hat, in silk grosgrain (a type of woven silk) still has one remaining practical use, as mentioned above under 'Very formal morning dress', where alternative court dress is described.

A hunting-weight silk hat

This is not a bad investment; if you can find one; in order to emulate Lord Ribblesdale. He was a great friend of Rosa Lewis, owner of the (old) Cavendish Hotel (whose life was dramatized as the Duchess of Duke Street), where he kept a permanent suite for use during periods of depression. King Edward VII described him as 'The Ancestor' owing to his imperious appearance, plainly visible in the National Portrait Gallery portrait of him.

The shells of hard hats are made from shellac which is a hardened paste derived from the secretions of the scale insect *Laccifer lacca*. It takes 150,000 insects to produce a pound of shellac. Its other uses include being a constituent of the polish used in French polishing for wood. To make a hard hat (Patey's is the very last English bespoke gentleman's hat maker) a wooden block is made and the shell of the hat is made over this by putting linen fabric (called goss) over the block. The goss will have been covered in the liquid shellac (called coodle) and left for several months to cure. After curing, the hat is shaped, trimmed and finished. Patey's use their own *conformateur* finally to shape the hat to the customer's head.

Grey silk top hat

This is known sometimes as a 'white hat' and is probably almost completely extinct in the original silk plush; although I suspect that HRH the Duke of

Grey felt top hat

Edinburgh has at least one. At one time, silk top hats were made in colours other than sleek black – on display in Lock's country room, there is a copper coloured silk top hat with a note which instructs the reader that it was once the pride and joy and very possibly the signature hat of a musical artist. It reads: 'Reward if Lost Return to: J Graham, personal address 6 Barnard Street, North 'land or local music hall Macdonald & Graham'.

Owing to a shortage of materials after the First World War, dove grey felt ones were made, by Lock's, specifically for Royal Ascot – and, of course, they still are made. Owners (except the young Winston Churchill) used to stow their hats at Lock's between Ascots. This was for preservation and to ensure that they were not sported out of season. All new modern offerings are in some form of felt. The felt shell is known as a 'drab shell'. There used to be such a thing as an Ascot suit too – basically a grey frock coat suit.

Nowadays, if a grey morning suit is worn to Ascot it includes a coat in the standard morning coat cut and a grey felt top hat. HRH The Prince of Wales seems to favour a black top hat with such a rig, whereas his father is more conventionally dressed in a black coat and grey top hat.

Hunting-weight Coke (bowler to most people)

This uniquely English hat (pronounced 'cook') was invented, in 1850, by Lock & Co. for a Mr Coke's gamekeepers (so that their hats would not be knocked off by branches when chasing poachers through the coverts and, presumably, would afford some measure of

A Coke or bowler hat

protection in any subsequent scuffle). Once it was thought to have been William Coke who ordered these hats but it has since been shown to be another member of the same family. However, the hats were later manufactured by South London hat makers called Bowler Brothers whose name has become ubiquitously eponymous – *except* at Lock's. It was once also (largely in the East End), called a 'billycock'; again (an irreverent) reference to the man who was once thought to have first commissioned them. These hats can look a bit 'Uncle Harry', especially if of inferior make. The cambridge (the

Lock's have a collection of conform cards showing the head shapes of the famous who bought their hats from them (including: French leader General Charles de Gaulle; novelist Evelyn Waugh, actor Charlie Chaplin, singer Frank Sinatra, surrealist artist Salvador Dali, actor Laurence, Lord Olivier, American icon Jackie Kennedy Onassis, the Duke of Windsor and the novelist Graham Greene. Oscar Wilde's last hat was bought there in 1895, just before his downfall. It was eventually paid for, by cheque, on the centenary of his death, in 2000. The artist, Mr Royston Du Maurier, who sent the cheque, said that he too had known 'feast and famine'. Lock's filed the cheque in the ledger showing his account. One can ask to see these records.

square-topped coke seen in some pictures of Sir Winston Churchill) is no longer available ready-made because people generally stopped buying them – probably when WSC died, although Lock's have supplied one in recent times.

Therefore, it is available (from Lock's) on a bespoke basis (presumably through Patey's) and which, in common with all ready-made hard hats, would be fitted after use of the famous Lock *conformateur*.

The town-weight Coke is seldom worn now. The character John Steed wore a variety of great examples of these hats in black, brown and grey (with very curly brims), to match his suits in the 1960s - 1970s television series *The Avengers*.

Homburg hat

This is a black, grey or brown felt hat, which is quite stiff. It has a curled brim, which is edged with ribbon and was introduced into this country by Edward VII who came across the style in the spa town of Homburg (the hats were originally manufactured at Bad Homburg). It was fully favoured until about 1922 when Scott's (formerly of 1 Old Bond Street now subsumed in Lock's) introduced

Homburg or Anthony Eden

the new snap brim felt hats which gradually took its place, although the Homburg did receive a second wind from Anthony Eden, sometime Foreign Secretary and then Prime Minister during the Suez Crisis of 1956. As a result of Eden's adoption of the style, the black version is sometimes now known as an 'Anthony Eden'.

Selection of soft felt hats

Borsalino soft felt·hat

These used to be readily available as bespoke too (in felts made out of beaver, hare and rabbit fur) but no longer. These hats are now ready-made, in standard sizes; just say 'borsalino'. The firm of **Borsalino** was established in 1857 in Alessandria, Italy, where they continue to make hats, including their famous felt hats, which are made out of Belgian rabbit fur. Their old works' site was so huge that it later formed the campus for the University.   There are different types of felt: it may come with a smooth finish, an antelope nap, brushed velour (sometimes called 'peach bloom') nap or a rough finish. I prefer the smooth type. I would say that one should have a black one for town, a grey one for travelling between town and country and a brown one for racing and maybe shooting. Wear these with the brim up for dignity or down to look like a punk hoodlum or a modern Hollywood actor. I rather like to pull the back left of the brim down, which is so very individual that I really do not recommend it to the unpractised. Avoid feather cockades in felt hats *at all costs*. Lock's also do a wide selection of brown felt styles, called the haydock, wetherby, sandown, chester (all excellent for racing – in fact, excellent for everywhere, except during Royal Ascot and at the Derby and Goodwood: for Goodwood a Panama hat is the thing).

Selection of tweed hats and caps

I suggest that you get these from Lock's or Herbert Johnson; there is a bespoke service available for them (remember Rex Harrison's rather modern cut checked hats?) and, of course, it would make sense to match country caps and sports' coats. Have one deerstalker for stalking deer in. As I sit here in the searing heat of Estado do Rio de Janeiro, a friend of mine is scrambling around the ling and furze in the Highlands of Scotland with his son after deer. So far, he has emailed me that he has 'missed two' – and probably got a real soaking into the bargain. However, he assures me that he was correctly dressed.

Cockades are, except in caps and deerstalkers, acceptable – but not necessary – in tweed hats. Apart from the green tyrolean hat, cockades are not usual in felt hats but people do sometimes wear them.

There are, of course, flat caps, sometimes known as 'cheese cutters' and 'baker's boys'. The tweed cap comes in many styles. They began as country headwear mainly worn by the working man until the extra full cut cap was worn by the Duke of Windsor, when Prince of Wales, who favoured the Lock & Co turnberry style, which is also worn by the present Prince of Wales. Lock & Co. caps are produced by Mr Gill who has made them for 30 years. His special development is called the Gill and is an extra-deep backed cap, designed to remain in place whatever the weather conditions. He produces the other full-cut Lock & Co. shapes, the turnberry and the sandwich – presumably ideal for a round of golf at the Royal St George's Golf Club, Sandwich Bay, Kent.

Superfino Monte Cristi Panama hat

Panama hat

These have never been made in Panama but in Ecuador and got the generic name 'panama' from the place where their international sale was first promoted through the workers on the Panama Canal (which was started by the French in 1880 but finished by the USA in 1914). Local bigwigs in Ecuador will not wear them, despite their high prestige in the West, because they rate them as lowly costume. Every new American President is given one by Ecuador. I am not sure whether, if re-elected, they get two. A top grade 20 llano weave of *jipijapa* fibre, made from the toquilla palm (*Carludovica palmata*), takes about two months to make by hand and costs – well it *costs*. Actually, it costs between £500 and £600 and when you consider all the export costs, the middlemen and so on, it is difficult not to feel sorry for the skilful soul sitting out there fashioning these things over eight weeks, for how much? Grade 20 means that there are 30 weaves of palm leaf per linear inch – you count the weaves in a linear inch and deduct 10 to give the grade. Grade 12 or 8 is normal and fairly acceptable but these are not *Superfinos*. The traditional high-crowned 'colonial style' *optimo* hats are also made in a form which may be folded away into a case for travelling but these have to have a cloth (rather than leather) inner band and consequently eventually show sweat marks. So, if you are off to somewhere very hot, don't opt for the folder style. The planter style is also dashing. The ordinary short-brimmed trilby looks a bit Uncle Harry – as indeed this style always does, whatever the material employed.

Green tyrolean hat

This is also known as an alpine hat. Have one of these and a badger brush cockade for Bavarian hunting. If you do this, the Loden cape could come in handy (perhaps, for hauling home shot Bavarians).

Sola topee

Please note that it is not sola*r* topee. This is a very light and useful sun hat, originally made from the pith of the sola tree (*Aeschynomene aspera*), covered in khaki or white coloured cloth and equipped with a leather chin strap which is normally folded up over the front of the brim. It has alternative names of pith helmet, sola

A modern Sola topee

topi and salacot. Modern versions are often made of cork (the bark of the Spanish cork oak, *Quercus suber*). This item has gone beyond mere twittery and become a great talking point. Sola topees are available again new from Lock's and Herbert Johnson (or sometimes second-hand from **Laurence Corner**). Gieves & Hawkes take the credit for the great range of this type of headgear which found its way to every corner of the former empire on military and civilian heads. Try to find the broader brimmed (African, rather than Indian) variety, since the narrower brimmed ones tend to share the description 'Uncle Harry' with short-brimmed trilby hats and

Astrakhan is also a city in Russia. The fur is also frequently known as Karakul and Persian lamb. It comes from a sheep which has been domesticated for well over a thousand years in central Asia and central Europe. Apparently, the best dark curled fur is taken from the foetus, which is procured by slaying the dam and is known as 'broadtail' or 'lambskin'. Presumably, local animal rights' activists (if any) see this as their equivalent of fox hunting.

cardigans. They also make one look rather as though one has a tortoise on one's head. In any event, if you want a full *puggaree* (a thin muslin scarf tied around to drape down and shield the back of the neck from tropical glare), you will probably need to improvise one yourself.

Fur jinnah caps

These are named after Mohammed Ali Jinnah who was first Governor-General of the new Pakistan (August 1947 until he died). He was known to his people as Quaid-e-Azam ('Great Leader'). Although a great nationalist and opponent of British rule in India, he nonetheless adopted some English tastes in dress and sported an eyeglass. The hats are in the style of a high forage cap and are properly made of astrakhan which comes from an oriental lamb with distinctively curly fur.

They are available in black, grey or brown. The best of the type come from Afghanistan and Pakistan – I have a fine brown one from Islamabad. However, home-manufactured varieties are available in the UK in a variety of furs, including sable, mink and musquash. What the domestic hats do not have in height to the crown, they make up for in price.

Stetson

Sometimes known as a 'Baden-Powell' (after the founder of the Scout movement who wore a high-crowned, wide-brimmed felt hat).

The original American version is a fairly hard high felt hat (with a curly brim) made by the **John B. Stetson Hat Company** which was founded, in 1865, by John B. Stetson with $10 worth of felt and some tools in a small rented room. From such unpromising beginnings were sprung the 'Hat of the West' and the 'Boss of the Plains'. The company is based in Garland, Texas, and they supply through links on their website. I recommend the current models: 'El Presidente' and 'El Patron'.

One of these is extremely useful for painting abroad, in the style of Churchill.

Straw boater

One could have one as an alternative to a panama, for use at Henley Royal Regatta and as a talking point (see also sola topee). They are traditionally worn with boat club or school or college colours in ribbon around the brim. They are also now retained as part of some school uniforms and at boating events – *and* they are still sometimes worn by butchers. Along with the ecru tropical dinner jacket, you will have to exercise your own judgement about how well it becomes you. The poet John Betjeman – not an especially dressy sort of chap, indeed rather scruffy generally – often favoured a boater.

Yachting cap

It is best to have one of these at the outset because, in time, it will prove just as indispensable as the opera hat, the homburg, the tyrolean hat, the straw boater, the sola topee, the jinnah cap and the stetson. However, you will probably have to bespeak it from Patey's. I have included a picture of Sir Arthur Quiller-Couch wearing one, probably on a committee vessel, during Fowey Royal Regatta before the Second World War. He was Commodore of the Royal Fowey Yacht Club, from 1911 until his death in 1944.

Whilst King Edward VII Professor of English Literature at Cambridge (1912–1944), he delivered a series of acclaimed lectures, some of which were later published as *On the Art of Writing* and *On the Art of Reading*. His lecture 'On Style' was delivered to a packed auditorium on Wednesday 28 January in the fateful year of 1914. I include here an extract – as its message has a general application:

"What is Style? What its . . . essence, the law of its being?

'Q' as Commodore of the Royal Fowey Yacht Club.

As I sat down to write this lecture, memory evoked a scene and with the scene a chance word of boyish slang, both of which may seem to you irrelevant until, or unless, I can make you feel how they hold for me the heart of the matter.

I once happened to be standing in a ball-room when there entered the most beautiful girl these eyes have ever seen or now – since they grow dull – ever will see. It was, I believe her first ball, and by some freak or in some premonition she wore black: and not pearls – which, I am told, maidens are wont to wear on these occasions – but one crescent of diamonds in her black hair. *Et vera incessu patuit dea* [And in her step, she was revealed a very goddess', from Virgil, *Aeneid* 1. 405] . . . Here, I say, was absolute beauty. It startled.

I think she was the most beautiful lady
That ever was in the West Country.
But beauty vanishes, beauty passes . . .

She died a year or two later. She may have been too beautiful to live long. I have a thought that she may also have been too good.

For I saw her with the crowd about her. I saw led up and presented among others the man who was to be, for a few months, her husband and then, as the men bowed pencilling on their programmes, over their shoulders I saw her eyes travel to an awkward young naval cadet (do you remember Crossjay in Meredith's The Egoist? It was just such a boy) who sat abashed and glowering sulkily beside me on the far bench. Promptly with a laugh, she advanced, claimed him, and swept him off into the first waltz.

When it was over he came back, a trifle flushed, and I felicitated him; my remark (which I forget) being no doubt 'just the sort of banality, you know, one does come out with' – as maybe that the British Navy kept its old knack of cutting out. But he looked at me almost in tears and blurted 'It isn't her beauty, sir. You saw? It's, it's – my God, it's the *style!*'

Now you may think that a somewhat cheap or at any rate inadequate cry of the heart in my young seaman; as you may think it inadequate in me, and moreover a trifle capricious to assure you (as I do) that the first and last secret of a good style consists in thinking with the heart as well as with the head."

He then goes on to explain the application of the general principle to the courtesy which a writer must show in easing the reader's way in reading a book.

The word 'style' is also frequently applied to dressing, but dressing is largely concerned with superficialities. A well-dressed man is not necessarily going to be a better-hearted fellow than a scruff but a man properly dressed for the time and place shows a consideration for those whom he encounters. In dress, that is 'just the proper style'. Moreover, if one wishes to see capital out of this, a well-dressed man elicits credit for the trouble that he has taken.

Chapter Nine

Second–Hand and Provincial Shops

Trust not the heart of that man for whom old clothes are not venerable. (Thomas Carlyle)

THERE have been several good attempts at establishing shops which deal in a wide range of good-quality second-hand men's clothing. However, with the exception of Laurence Corner and those at www.thechap.net, even the very good attempts (that I know of) do not seem to last very long and so we are left with various other possible sources. However, it must be borne in mind that these sources of second-hand goods are, obviously, not going to make or order anything for you – although you might be able to persuade the owners to give you first refusal on stuff that comes their way. Accordingly, there is little point in going too far out of your way.

First of all, there are charity shops. I recommend frequenting those in the most prosperous areas – in London this means those such as Victoria, Belgravia, Kensington and Chelsea, Marylebone, Bloomsbury, Blackheath, Dulwich and Hampstead and Highgate (I don't recall any in St James's, Piccadilly or Mayfair as such), where you are most likely to find real bargains – and it must not be underestimated that you will, from time to time, find them: things like vintage evening top coats, morning coats, evening coats and dinner jackets, blazers, Sulka ties and even silk toppers. However, it is best to go into them without looking for a particular item and just let yourself be surprised with what you do find. I once came across a grey morning coat in a charity shop in Westminster. Inside the breast pocket was the name of a deceased press baron. However, the coat was definitely the wrong size for me.

Then there is e-bay on which I have bought various things and, apart from a small percentage of chisellers, people who ply their wares there seem to be honest and eager to please. However, so far as second-hand clothing is concerned, it is best to be able to inspect the wares first – both for condition and fit. Even then, there may be surprises. I recall a friend of the family returning, in the 1960s, from a business trip to Chicago with a very sharp second-hand suit – no doubt advertised as 'nearly new' – which he had quickly tried on, found it to fit and he picked it up for very little. After wearing it a couple of times, someone pointed out that there were what, on closer inspection, looked like a couple of bullet holes in the back of the coat.

Then, as mentioned, there are army surplus stores all over the place, which, from time to time, stock well-made items (in good condition), which with a change of buttons can very often be passed off as, say, safari outfits for just a few pounds. There is not much point in recommending anywhere in particular because they all stock very similar stuff and all also have a high turnover. However, most districts of London and large provincial centres have these shops and they are certainly worth an occasional visit.

Not quite second-hand, but in the same spirit: obviously makers of all categories of bespoke clothes sometimes have them left on their hands. People die before they collect them – or disappear. Some shops actively market these uncollected items once a year in a sale; others do not *openly* market them but are quite happy to part with them for some much reduced price once it has become clear that the person for whom they were intended is a definite 'no show'. I did once manage to secure something worthwhile from New & Lingwood in one of their sales of such items. It was just after the Falklands War in 1982 and an Argentinian customer had told them (probably in Spanish) what they could do with a pair of great evening pumps, which he had bespoken from them just before the Argentinian invasion of the Falklands. The Iron Lady (Margaret Thatcher) got her Finest Hour – and I got a pair of first-rate, slim-line pumps for something like a fifth of their bespoke cost.

University Town and Provincial Suppliers

I list below some university town and provincial suppliers for those times when one happens to be out of town and in urgent need of an item. However, it must be said that most things can be sent by FEDEX.

Oxford

David Clarke,
19 Broad Street,
Oxford
OX1 4BX
(tel. 01865 242698).

Castell & Sons
(University Outfitters),
13 Broad Street,
Oxford
OX1 3AS
(tel. 01865 244000).

Cambridge

A.E. Clothier
(University and General Outfitter),
5A Pembroke Street,
Cambridge
CB2 3QY
(tel. 01223 354339).

Ede & Ravenscroft
71–72 Trumpington Street,
Cambridge
CB2 1RJ
(tel. 01223 350048).

Eton

New & Lingwood,
118 High Street,
Eton, Windsor
SL4 6AN
(tel. 01753 866286).

Joseph Gane,
125 High Street,
Eton, Windsor
SL4 6AN
(tel. 01753 866284).

Exeter

Damien Carberry,
30 Princesshay,
Exeter
EX1 1NB
(tel: 01392 217847).

Cody Outfitters,
111–113 Fore Street,
Exeter
EX4 3JF
(tel. 01392 213880).

Bristol

Case & Edwards,
27 Zetland Road,
Bristol
BS6 7AH
(tel. 0117 942 4870).

Birmingham

Rosen & Nathan,
17 Cannon Street,
Birmingham
B2 5EN
(tel. 0121 643 4834).

Gieves & Hawkes
The Mailbox,
44-46 Wharfside Street
Birmingham
B1 1RE
(tel. 0121 632 5295).

York

C.E. Seymour,
10 Bootham,
York
YO30 7BL
(tel. 01904 653148).

Edinburgh

Gieves & Hawkes,
at Harvey Nichols,
30–34 St Andrew's Square,
Edinburgh
EH2 2AD
(tel. 0132 524 8388).

Portsmouth

Gieves & Hawkes,
Unit 57,
Gunwharf Quays,
Portsmouth Harbour
PO1 3TU
(tel. 01239 282 6648).

Winchester

Gieves,
1–2 The Square,
Winchester
SO23 9ES
(tel. 01962 852096).

Chapter Ten

Some Accessories

R ain sounds so much better on silk, sir. (Swaine Adeney Brigg umbrella salesman, *c.*1986)

UMBRELLAS, STICKS, HUNTING WHIPS

NOT EXACTLY apparel unless you are a veteran Guards' officer but included anyway to go with the Topper and Coke, (or 'Bowler'). Swaine Adeney Brigg's do the only new silk umbrellas but I am afraid that they seem to me to have gone *slightly* downhill since they sold me my first (from their former, palatial emporium next to Fortnum & Mason's in Piccadilly) which I bespoke in combined silver-mounted rosewood handle and horn ferrule (tip), after the incredible but irresistible sales line, recorded at the head of this chapter. They just do not seem as substantial as they used to.

Whangee handles (from bamboo of the genus *Phyllostachys*) are, after a period when imports (from China) dried up, available again (tightly curled, knotty cane root like Steed had in *The Avengers* – I mean the proper Patrick Macnee version) and I'd go to **James Smith & Sons Ltd.** Look for a piece with a good tight curl of reasonable thickness and with an even distribution of sections between the ridges where the sucker roots have been trimmed. Under no circumstances must this be allowed to remain wet or in any extreme ambient temperature, for fear that it will uncurl; therefore, do not, for example, leave it in the rear window of a car or in a porch or an orchid house.

I think that Ralph Fiennes had a solid hickory-shafted Brigg in the more recent *Avengers* film. One point about umbrellas and the country: apart from church, formal occasions in provincial towns

Ebony is the heartwood of Macassar ebony (*Diospyrus celebica*) or the blackest wood of all, Gabon ebony (*Diospyrus crassiflora*). There are other types and some have a brownish or a greenish streak.

There are several types of rosewood, including: Burmese (*Dalbergia olivera*), Honduran (*Dalbergia stevensonii*) and that from Madagascar (*Dalbergia baronii*). Its common name derives from its scent, rather than its colour.

Snakewood is so-called from the snakeskin-like pattern of its grain and it is also used in musical instrument making. Its scientific name is *Piratinera guianensis*. This comes from Surinam.

Violet wood is otherwise known as kingwood and violetta. Its scientific name is *Dalbergia cearensis* – it is a type of rosewood.

and golf, umbrellas are not used in the country. Illustrated is a splendid selection of whole hardwood umbrellas made by James Smith. The woods range from ebony, to rosewood, snakewood and violet wood.

Umbrella derives from the latin umbra, meaning 'shade'. There is evidence that the Etruscans had something of the kind (from ancient vases); also that they were known in Nineveh (from sculptures). The

James Smith & Sons whole hardwood umbrellas (i.e. from the handle to the tip, they are constructed from a single piece of hardwood).

Chinese claim to have invented the first of the kind in the parasol, during the ancient Xia Dynasty. They were probably the first to wax the paper to waterproof it against rain. There is also some evidence that the Greeks had them. Some societies have reserved such appliances for their royal families and some have granted only women the privilege of freely using them. In Bengal, even common people used a type made from the leaves of *Licerata peltata* from early times. The use of the umbrella in England in modern times is said to have begun with Jonas Hanway (a traveller and founder of the Magdalen Hospital) in the mid-Eighteenth Century. However, in the novel, dated 1719, Daniel Defoe has Robinson Crusoe make an umbrella device for himself on his island. They were not terribly popular at first and a John MacDonald relates in 1770 that, when he ventured forth with an umbrella, he was greeted with the shout 'Frenchman, Frenchman, why don't you call a coach?' Originally the frames were made of wood or whalebone and the first umbrella shop to open in England was James Smith & Sons in 1830. Samuel Fox invented the steel-ribbed variety in 1852, as a way of usefully disposing of surplus farthingale stays (corset stays), the manufacture of which was part of his principal business. The unrelated Fox Umbrellas Ltd, originally founded in 1868, still exists. They made the John Steed sword umbrellas for the television series. Other names for an umbrella are 'Hanway' (after Jonas Hanway); 'Gamp' (after Charles Dickens' Sarah Gamp) and 'Brolly' (a diminutive). Apparently, Americans say 'Bumbershoot' – which appears to be a combination of a corruption of umbra and 'shoot' as in parachute. Not always the bland item that it first seems, the Bulgarian dissident Georgi Ivanov Markov was assassinated with a ricin-tipped umbrella on Waterloo Bridge in 1978. Sometimes they are truly symbolic and their proper use is totally forgotten. I know someone whose father was head of a Quango and one day, in the 1980s, the son saw his father, with mac, hat and umbrella caught in a shower. The father tucked his umbrella under his mac, grasped his hat – and made a spirited dash for cover.

I'd also go to Smith's for old and new sticks and canes. A formal day cane would be a silver- or gold-topped Malacca cane with a horn ferrule. (Malacca, mottled or 'clouded' yellow through brown even to reddish, is made from the stem of the palm *Calamus scipionum*; native to China, Sumatra and Malaysia.) A formal evening stick would be made of ebony wood with a gold or silver top and a horn ferrule. Besides Whangee, Malacca cane is quite acceptable on an umbrella. Generally, the best pieces of Malacca are nicely mottled (clouded) and have quite a pronounced growing ridge down one side: on an umbrella this would acceptably appear on the lower side.

Michael German in Kensington High Street does a line in ornate antique sticks but very few have any provenance as to former ownership – so you are investing in art if you go there, for the sake of what Brummell would have called 'the nice conduct of a clouded cane' .

In the age of convenience and small motor cars, now only the infirm really carry canes and sticks. However, from earliest times, mankind has carried a piece of wood: originally, of course, as a spear and staff in one. Gradually, they became status symbols. The correct etiquette with a stick or cane (or, indeed, an umbrella) is: never drag it, run it along railings or grating, tuck it under your arm, wave it in the air or (unless you really need it as a support) lean upon it, when standing. It should just rest lightly on the ground.

A word on hunting whips: get one now (preferably an old one made by Brigg or Swaine or Swaine Adeney Brigg, depending on how old it is – until the Second World War, Swaine and Brigg were separate businesses). Very good examples will have a stag horn handle (sometimes with a crown button), silver collar and a cane or steel shaft. This is often covered in braided leather with a keeper at the end for the thong to thread through. The thong is the business part of the whip and is plaited leather. At the end of the thong is the lash. The colour of the lash varies from hunt to hunt. It is used to shoo hounds away from your horse's feet. If you do not act now you will probably soon be caught by a statute altogether banning their manufacture. There is a website which does a roaring trade in equestrian paraphernalia, including hunting whips (www.sportingcollection.com).

BUTTONHOLES

According to his daughter, Lilias, Sir Henry Rider Haggard (author of many adventure books including *King Solomon's Mines*, as well as various government reports), used to wear a rose (hybrid tea roses

The name of orchids (*Orchidaceae*) derives from the Greek for testicle – owing to the shape of some flowers. There are 25,000 species and also hybrids on top of that. They are largely epiphytic (in that they grow on trees, but are not parasites) or lithophytic (in that they grow on rocks). Another great man for orchids was politician Joseph Chamberlain (father of Austen and Neville) who wore one every waking moment – but he *did* have a botanist on his staff to superintend their culture in vast orchid houses. A specialist supplier of orchids and requisites is **McBean's Orchids.**

are favoured as they have neat tight buds) or carnation (the clove varieties are scented) in summer and an orchid in winter.

From a photograph of Haggard, gardenias also featured (*gardenia jasminoides* is a good one). However, gardenias are not generally available as cut flowers and you will have to buy (or cultivate) a flowering bush. They are very temperamental plants in that they need a warm, humid atmosphere, just the right amount of soft water (disliking hard water and alkaline soil) and are susceptible to scale insect infestation and to dropping their buds suddenly. Moreover, to flower successfully, they need a minimum night temperature of 50 degrees Fahrenheit.

Noel Coward is sadly on record as saying that only a stationmaster would wear a rose in his buttonhole. Here, I confess that I am resolutely against him for a number of reasons:

Despite Oscar Wilde's famous dictum that 'a well conceived buttonhole is the only true connection between art and nature' – one small word about *arranged* buttonholes (i.e. a flower combined, by means of green paper-covered wire, with fern fronds): this is the suburban and provincial florist's idea of a wedding buttonhole. If offered one by, or on behalf of, the father of the bride or by the groom, it would be the height of bad manners to refuse it or, having accepted it, fussy beyond belief thereafter to interfere with it – but a useful pre-emptive strike is to make sure that you wear your own plain buttonhole.

- The example of Sir H. Rider Haggard
- Station masters were generally very smart and useful people (whose demise like that of train guards – replaced by 'chief conductors' and, worse, 'revenue protection officers' – is greatly to be regretted)
- Roses should be worn by an Englishman at least on St George's Day (23 April), although, traditionally, in one's hatband
- Out of deference to someone I know who, for decades, used to grow roses the year round (under glass) and everyday wore one in his buttonhole

There are various flowers for other occasions and people – most importantly: cornflowers for Old Harrovians; primroses for Disraeli's birthday; artificial poppies for Remembrance Day;

Gardenia jasminoides: *the photograph is from Clifton Nurseries.*

gardenias for ordinary morning dress or full fig evening dress, for which white carnations are a poor substitute and white camellias of *camellia japonica*, although unscented, a better; deep red clove carnations go with a dark suit or black tie.

The Prince of Wales seems to wear an array of tiny flowers which probably grow organically in his Highgrove garden – but since they are so tiny, we do not know what they are! Still, it is fairly spirited to wear a buttonhole at all in modern Britain.

Necessary other accessories

I do not cover in detail, watches, or touch at all on pens. However, keep everything you wear simple and discreet. Certain things are essential. Have a pair of oblong or oval gold cufflinks for the day and, say, a pair of round or oblong mother-of-pearl cufflinks for the evening (maybe with a small ruby in the centre). You will also need a pearl pin for formal day wear and building a collection of others makes sense. For evening shirtfront studs, have plain pearl. You will need a long safety pin style of stock pin for hunting. Don't forget that you will need front and back collar studs for shirts with detachable collars. These you can get second-hand in gold; however, frankly, the modern versions which shirt-makers sell are practical and sensible. I suggest selecting a front collar stud called the 'bayonet' because it is pointed and much easier to insert than a round-headed stud. For the precious metal items, either you will have inherited some or you can buy them relatively cheaply from jewellers who deal in second-hand goods – such as many shops in the Burlington Arcade and Camden Passage. Just stroll up and down and peer in the windows where they tend to display most of their current stock; however, you will have to go in and inquire about prices because these are seldom displayed.

I do not intend to go too far into the vast subject of toiletries here, but a word or two about colognes is not wholly out of place. Floris 'Special 127' formula (the name derives from the page number in the formula book) was originally made up for Russian Grand Duke Orloff in 1890 and has, subsequently, been favoured by such different people as Eva Peron ('Evita') and Noel Coward. Ian

Floris was founded in Jermyn Street, by Juan Famenias Floris, a Menorcan, in 1730, as a comb-maker and barber. This family firm still flourishes, now specializing in scents and colognes. It received its first royal warrant from George IV in 1820 (as a smooth pointed comb-maker). Since then it has held 16 royal warrants. Some of its other customers included Florence Nightingale OM (1820–1910) – the 'Lady with the Lamp' – who made nursing into a serious profession; Mary Shelley (1797-1851) who wrote Frankenstein; Rosa Lewis, 'The Duchess of Duke Street'; and Beau Brummell himself. Although I have mentioned that John Lobb's may be the most beautiful shop in the world, the Floris shop (smaller but older and perfectly preserved) is also a contender for the title, with its mahogany cabinets and counter, bought from the Great Exhibition of 1851.

Fleming (and, through him, James Bond) used 'No. 89' created in 1955 – the name derives from the Floris street number in Jermyn Street.

Taylor of Old Bond Street's 'No. 74' (*their* street number in Jermyn Street) and Taylor's 'Victorian Limes' are also highly recommended. Taylor's does a great range of shaving soaps – both in a tube and in cake form, including one which is almond-scented. **G. Trumper,** originally of Curzon Street but now also in Jermyn Street, supplies an excellent extract of limes too which comes with a pink label. During the First World War they ran out of the original green paper and so substituted what was available – pink; they kept with it ever afterwards, maybe as a small act of remembrance for all those men who would never return to have their hair trimmed there again. Creed Green Irish Tweed was formulated especially for Cary Grant and is available from **Les Senteurs** – along with others in the range, including Creed Royal English Leather. Another famous cologne is by **Czech & Speake** who also make an aftershave. **Pinaud** Elixir is a famous hair preparation; they also make an excellent bay rum and their own version of essence of limes.

Chapter Eleven

Some Named Events and Activities

T he well-dressed man is he whose clothes
you never notice.
(W. Somerset Maugham)

ROYAL ASCOT WEEK

TO GET INTO the royal enclosure for the
first time (by application to the Royal
Enclosure Office), you used to need to be
sponsored by someone who had been there four
times before. However, according to rule
changes, soon you will be able to buy your way
in – even here. If, despite the new grandstand
(which some maintain provides, of course in the
modern way, more for corporate entertaining
than race-going and viewing), you go, I suggest
the following. For Royal Ascot, bring together
the black morning coat, hound's-tooth trousers
and formal white day waistcoat. Make sure
that you have a plain white shirt with a stiff
fold-down detachable collar to which you will
bring a silver woven silk tie and pearl pin.
Top it all off with a silk black or grey topper
(black used to be traditional on Ladies' Day
– the Thursday), chamois gloves and plain
black calf oxford shoes (or galosh-topped
shoes or boots if you have them). In my

*W. Hall Walker, horse
breeder, dressed appropriately
for Royal Ascot.*

view, gloves, like hats and handkerchiefs are symbols of civilization; however, few people wear gloves to formal occasions nowadays, even to Royal Ascot. A gardenia is the correct flower – and make sure that you carry a good silk-covered umbrella to keep it all dry.

HENLEY ROYAL REGATTA, WIMBLEDON AND COWES WEEK

What better opportunity to marry up your blazer or reefer jacket and white ducks or white flannels, your co-respondent shoes, a white shirt, tie or cravat and a panama hat or boater? Although, at Cowes, you will need some white rubber-soled deck shoes (for such rarefied things, you should take yourself off to a bespoke establishment) and you *must*, of course, give the yachting cap an airing. At Henley, you may also wear any rowing colours to which you are entitled.

Henley Royal Regatta was started by the Henley Local Corporation in 1839 as a tourist attraction on the Thames and has been held ever since, except during the wars. Its first royal patron was Prince Albert, in the year of the Great Exhibition (1851). There have been four different courses. That in use today is the Straight Course, laid out in 1924 and is 1 mile and 550 yards long and 80 feet wide, beginning on the Berkshire side of Temple Island and finishing at Poplar point. There are two crews

Reginald Saumarez de Havilland, dressed for boating.

in each heat. The Stewards' Enclosure is open to members and their guests only and a strict dress code applies. The Mile & an Eighth Restaurant is extremely popular so remember: book early! The rig suggested above for this occasion will, if you otherwise qualify for entrance, ensure your admittance. The Regatta Enclosure is open to all, subject to payment and, although there is no strict dress code, many observe the spirit of the occasion. The event is normally held in late June or early July for five days, from Wednesday to Sunday.

The All England Lawn Tennis Club Championships is held six weeks before the first Monday in August and is on grounds run by the All England Croquet and Lawn Tennis Club in Wimbledon, London SW19.

Cowes Week is eight days of yacht racing in the Solent, at the beginning of August, arranged by the Royal Yacht Squadron. This is a yacht club founded in a St James' tavern on 1 June 1815, with membership open to owners with yachts over 10 tons. The Prince Regent became a member in 1817 and, when he ascended the throne in 1820, 'Royal' was added to the name of the club. The regatta began properly in 1826 and George IV gave a gold cup for the occasion. The name the Royal Yacht *Squadron* dates from 1833.

The game of tennis arguably originated with the Egyptians – in friezes on temple walls a ball game is depicted. It came to Europe with the Moors and fascinated the monks who called it *la soule*. In the Twelfth and Thirteenth Centuries it came out of the monasteries and a glove and handle supplanted the bare hand. Balls became made of leather stuffed with bran instead of wood and in the Sixteenth to Eighteenth Centuries it was a game much favoured in France where it was called *Jeu de paume*, palm game. Play was started with the cry 'Tenez!' It was a favoured game with royal courts and 'real tennis' was played off the walls (there is a 'real tennis' court at Hampton Court Palace). At the first Wimbledon tournament there were 22 players and 200 spectators. The last time men wore long trousers on court was in 1939.

Throughout the week there are dinners, dances, cocktail parties and concerts and on the final Friday there is a great display of fireworks. Important races are for the America's Cup (first raced and won by the America in 1851), the Admiral's Cup the Queen's Cup, the Britannia Cup and the New York Challenge Cup. The Fastnet Race is held only in odd numbered years as it is so perilous.

TWICKENHAM

Here one should wear cords, a jumper, the Barbour, a cap and stout country shoes. Twickenham Stadium ('Twickers') is the home of Rugby Union football and is in Middlesex. It was built on ground formerly used for the cultivation of cabbages and so sometimes is also called 'Cabbage Patch'. The first international there was on 15 January 1910 between England and Wales. Rugby football is supposed to have been invented by a bored schoolboy at Rugby School in Warwickshire, as commemorated by a plaque in the school, which was founded in 1567 by the will of Lawrence Sheriff, originally to educate the poor of the area. It is now one of England's major public schools. Its most famous headmaster was Dr Thomas Arnold (1795–1842) who introduced enlightened reforms in education, emphasizing sport, self-control, reliability, steadfastness and taught the assumption of responsibility which, altogether, proved a combination that has since been adopted in education systems throughout the world.

BALLS

Follow the dress code on the invitation to a ball. In fact, whenever a dress code is indicated by the hosts, follow it. On those occasions when an invitation for *any* event is silent, either ask the hosts or, if that is not practicable, imagine what they will be wearing. Although it is best to be dressed exactly right, *remember that it is always better to be under-dressed rather than over-dressed; because the person who will be feeling most self-conscious if you are under-dressed is – you.* You can always fib lightly and say that you were unavoidably detained and, 'rather than dress and be late, I came as I am'. These days, even to black tie events, sometimes men turn up in dark lounge suits, black shoes and dark ties. In fact, a good dark lounge suit will, at a pinch, pass muster *almost* anywhere. However, obviously, a lounge suit is not going to do at a white tie event or for the Royal Enclosure at Ascot (unless you are Rex Harrison and happen to be just in a film – like *My Fair Lady*).

There are some balls arranged privately (most notably the University Balls) but Queen Charlotte's Ball and such like are no longer held and there is no official control of what events are, or are not, a part of the season (to the extent that it survives at all). There is a group called The London Season, which holds itself out as representing Society and arranges functions for wannabees. The champagne house of Veuve Cliquot publishes annual cards on which *its* idea of the London Season is promulgated (as well as an advertisement for its wares).

FISHING

Take the shooting option below but substitute a tweed hat (on which to store your hand-tied fishing flies) for the cap or brown felt hat; knee breeches for the plus twos and you will need waders which you can find at **Farlow's** in

Arthur Diosy, orientalist, in full fig for a ball.

Pall Mall and the Royal Opera Arcade.

Fishing seasons in the UK are (the exact dates depend on the river): for salmon between January and November; for brown trout between March and October; for sea trout also between March and October. Before undertaking this pursuit, you should acquaint yourself with the current law, including the need for licences, for the water in question.

SHOOTING

Wear a shooting suit, probably a tweed coat and plus twos knickerbockers, perhaps greaves or gaiters, stout country shoes (or wellies or Newmarket boots) and a cap or narrow-brimmed brown felt hat. Although I have mentioned Barbours, a seriously good tweed should withstand all weathers in which shooting is likely to be even marginally *enjoyable*.

HUNTING

The clothing for this is specifically covered in considerable detail in the Country Chapter. The foxhunting season is from the beginning of November to the beginning of April. I do not deal with stag hunting and hare coursing. Curiously, the Hunting with Dogs [sic] Act 2004 would seem to permit the hunting of a rabbit

Lord Savile, dressed for shooting, including long gaiters over his lower legs.

with a pack of hounds or even with three or more 'dogs'. Is Brer Rabbit not cuddlier than Reynard? Or was the purpose of the statute nothing more than an overt exercise in 'class discrimination' by urban inverted snobs? I venture no opinion but would suggest a careful perusal of the relevant legislation before undertaking any hunting activity.

The open seasons for game are, except where otherwise stated, for England and Wales and are as follows:

pheasant between 1 October and 1 February;

partridge between 1 September and 1 February;

wildfowl (inland) between 1 September and 31 January;

wildfowl (below high water mark) between 1 September and 20 February;

grouse (Scotland) between 12 August (the 'Glorious 12th') and 10 December;

ptarmigan (Scotland) between 12 August and 10 December;

common snipe (jack snipe being protected) between 12 August and 31 January;

woodcock between 1 October and 31 January;

blackgame between 20 August and 10 December;

golden plover between 1 September and 31 January.

The *closed season* for hare is between 1 March ('mad as a March hare') and 31 July. Pigeon and rabbits are not game and they enjoy no closed season.

For stalking deer (here described in Scotland only) the seasons are:

red deer stags, between 1 July and 20 October;

the hinds, between 21 October and 15 February;

fallow bucks, between 1 August and 30 April, does between 21 October and 15 February;

roe bucks, between 1 April and 20 October, does between 21 October and 31 March.

Before undertaking these pursuits, you should acquaint yourself with the current law, including the need for licences, for the place in question.

Arthur James, in hunting scarlet, for a day with the hunt.

RACING

Usual dress to informal racing is a tweed or summer suit and a brown racing felt hat (or, at Goodwood, a Panama). I am reliably informed that the racing felt hat also comes in green and blue. For spectating at point to points, you might well be able to wear the outfit described for Twickenham. Long, long gone are the days when men wore little Dutch dolls on the brims of their black toppers (covered with a green veil) to the Derby; however, those closely involved with the horses (owners, trainers and heavy backers) tend to wear morning dress to the Derby (with a black coat) and a black topper – all as for Ascot, except *never* wear a grey topper, even to the Cheltenham Gold Cup (only wear one to Ascot). If you wear a grey topper to your *wedding*, you deserve to have your stag night photographs posted on the internet.

GOLF

For this, plus fours used to be *the thing*. However, very few people play in these now and you need to be at least a reasonably good golfer to get away with them (or play at dawn by yourself) and the usual trousers are boldly checked. Team these up with a jumper to match the weather, golf shoes, a cap and a golf glove (from Pickett). Of course, you will need a large golfing umbrella. Oddly enough, the Porter's Lodge at Lincoln's Inn sells excellent golfing umbrellas –

and at a very reasonable price. They are violet and white and emblazoned with a badge of the Inn. However, they seem to be on sale to all comers.

Golf is originally a Scottish game and so purists pronounce it 'goff'. In 1452 James II of Scotland banned the game for a time because playing it was distracting his archers from their practice. Mark Twain described the game as 'a good walk spoiled'. Blackheath was the first club established in England – that is, the first outside Scotland.

SPECTATING CRICKET

For suitable clothing (wherever you are sitting), see Henley and Wimbledon above. The MCC tie is *de rigueur* for members at Lord's. Apart from the famously garish version there is a quieter model in dark blue with the MCC motif. Benson & Clegg used to sell very well-made MCC ties, until the MCC created such a fuss over intellectual property rights in the design that Benson & Clegg, disdaining such petty disputes, cut all their stock of these ties in half and binned them. The only versions of this tie available now are the ones sold by the club.

There is also (believe it or not) an MCC blazer in the same orange and mustard colours; the club will even sell you the cloth to have your own blazer made up. The fathers wearing morning dress to watch the Eton v Harrow cricket match has fallen into desuetude, as has exuberantly bashing out the top of your topper at the close of play (in any event, as with the Incas' ancient practice of slaughtering shorn wild vicunas, there would now be serious conservation issues at stake).

There is evidence, from court records relating to a land dispute, that cricket was played in England in the Sixteenth Century. It was probably played much earlier as a bat and ball game. There is also an ancient Indian game, still played, called *Gulle Danda* (Punjabi for 'ball' and 'stick') from which the modern game may also, in part, derive. The old French *criquet* means 'club' and is the origin of the name for croquet which may be related to cricket.

OPERA AND BALLET, THEATRE AND CONCERTS

Apart from Glyndebourne (when black tie is expected) and gala events (when dress will, in any event, be specified), for these, no one wears evening dress anymore and, sadly, few people even wear a suit. If they do, they hardly ever even wear a tie. I suggest that a dark lounge suit and dark tie is generally appropriate.

The opera at Glyndebourne was begun by the hereditary owner of the house, John Christie, who built an organ room and held amateur concerts there in the 1920s. To improve the quality of the entertainment, he engaged a professional opera singer (Audrey Mildmay) whom he subsequently married. They decided to do something on a grander scale while they were touring opera houses of Europe on their honeymoon. They built an opera house large enough to present Mozart's intimate operas. It opened on 28 May 1934 with a performance of *Le Nozze di Figaro*. The opera house was enlarged several times until it was replaced by an entirely new building (paid for largely by donation). This opened 60 years to the day after the first ever performance and the first performance in the new house was – again – *Le Nozze di Figaro*.

The Royal Opera House, Covent Garden, is now home to the Royal Opera and the Royal Ballet. The façade and the auditorium date from the 1858 construction. The rest dates from a reconstruction in the 1990s. It began as the Theatre Royal Covent Garden by Letters Patent granted on his restoration by Charles II to Sir William Davenant. A new building went up on the site of a former *convent garden* in 1728 for John Rich. All the modern greats of opera and ballet have appeared here.

RESTAURANTS AND CASINI

Traditionalists would wear a dark lounge suit and dark tie. Evening dress is not out of place but would be confined to occasions after having just been somewhere else where it was actually required. Modernists would omit the tie with a suit; presumably in an attempt to ape (and ape is the word) some modern Britons who see themselves as leaders of fashion. Sadly, this is accepted by many establishments, except some top end hotels and casini where, as in St James's Club land, a coat and tie are still required.

I have been criticized for using the Italian plural (casino means 'little house') rather than the Standard English plural of 'casinos'. I don't care; especially since *casini* was good enough for Anthony Powell in *To Keep the Ball Rolling*, part of his great autobiographical *Dance to the Music of Time*.

CHURCH

For attendance at church, a mid-grey flannel suit, light shirt and discreet tie are appropriate for town; maybe substituting a restrained tweed suit for the country: with black or brown shoes, as the case may require. There is nothing wrong with dark brown or oxblood coloured shoes with a mid-grey flannel suit in the country.

IF YOU END UP IN THE DOCK

If, after revelry, you are unfortunate enough to end up before the Beak, wear a very dark suit, white shirt, sombre tie (*under no circumstances, a bow tie*), black shoes and (if you are guilty or found guilty – not necessarily the same thing) a very contrite expression indeed. If it happens in the same court twice, try to wear a look of being a little insane too; sporting an odd pair of shoes (i.e. one black and one brown) might help. On the subject of odd shoes; according to Brian Dobbs' *And the Last Shall be First*, the late Eric Lobb was once summoned to a fitting of shoes for an esteemed customer at the Palace and, with more haste and less speed, found himself in a cab going thither wearing a combination of odd shoes (quite what he, as a shoe-maker, was doing *shoeless* immediately before he was summoned is not stated).

IF YOU ARE INVOLVED IN THE CIVIL COURTS

Follow the directions in the immediately preceding entry. However, if you think that you have a good case, you *might* wear a sombre bow tie as a way of cocking a snook at the other side.

Chapter Twelve

Care of Clothing

A stitch in time saves nine.

SUITS, SHIRTS AND TIES

GOOD CLOTHES should last a long time. Sometimes they last more than one lifetime. Former Prime Minister Harold Macmillan ('Our people have never had it so good') passed on a suit that he had had made as a young man to his grandson. Shoes also can last that long. But you must look after them properly. Dry cleaning suits and coats (indeed anything) is better avoided. The alternatives are sponging and pressing or steam cleaning. Even hanging a suit overnight in a steamed-up bathroom removes creases. When choosing suit and trouser hangers, bear in mind that there are some on the market which have a toothed rubber grip to keep the trousers in place and stop them rolling off to form untidy heaps of crumpled cloth on the floor of your wardrobe. If you do any pressing yourself, remember to place brown paper or damp cotton between the iron and the cloth or you will make the cloth shine. Having a couple of good clothes brushes is a good investment and it is as well to have one soft and one harder, as well as a soft wire brush, together with a suede brush. Laundering of shirts is fairly self-evident, whether done at home or at a laundry. Strictly speaking, shirtsleeves should not have creases in them but this is difficult to achieve without a second miniature ironing board and a good deal of patience.

Most people hang their ties for storage. However, it is far better to roll them up and store them in a drawer. This means that the weight of the ties does not pull them down and cause creases and stretching of the patterns. However, it is always important to make sure that the creases from wearing a tie have dropped out before storing away the tie.

SHOES

Whether your shoes are bespoke or not, always use trees when storing them. However, do not put the trees in until the shoes have rested and thoroughly dried out inside. Try also to give shoes at least a complete day of rest between outings. Obviously, use the maker's own polish and remember to polish under the instep on the part called the 'shank' – situated between the heel and the main part of the sole. I even do the soles, which annoys people with light-coloured carpets, although this is not my principal reason for doing it – it is very protective of the leather. It is helpful sometimes to use leather cream (available from any good shoe-maker) on the inside leather because this helps to prevent cracking. Before going out in the cold in patent leather and to stop these shoes cracking, place them into a warm oven for a few minutes but be careful that you do not cook them – not least because, apart from the expense, it would

make the most horrible smell. Bespoke shoes often come with their own bags and it is as well to keep them in these. One most important point is that you must not keep shoes in a very dry centrally heated atmosphere or they will disintegrate. In Brazil I have another problem to cope with, that of tropical mildew, which may or may not be associated with the heavy summer layers of algae in the sea across the road. There is also what the Brazilians call *maresia* – the salt-laden wind, which corrodes and destroys almost all that it touches. Always take shoes and boots back to their actual maker for repairs and never, ever, *ever* go to heel bars.

You will find that a suede rubber (available from any good shoe-maker) is important in the removal of surface scuffs and marks from suede and buckskin.

GLOVES

Chamois and mocha (sheepskin) gloves can be washed in Lux soap flakes. Just wear the gloves and make to wash your hands. Rinse out the soap and carefully take them off and lay them flat in a cool dry place to dry out. Do not put wet gloves on any kind of heater or they will become like giant crinkly poppadoms.

HATS

Felt and tweed hats can be steamed to refresh the fabric and to reinstate the shape. Just hold the hat at a safe distance in a stream of steam from a pot or a kettle and gently brush it up. I mention below that white vinegar is good for cleaning Panamas. A silk topper can be brushed with a hat brush and also shone up with a velvet pad. Occasionally (especially if the silk gets spotted with rain) you will need to take it to a hatter to be ironed. Proper hatters can also reblock soft hats to bring back the shape.

STAINS AND MARKS

Why is it that it is always the new Hermes tie which attracts the gravy so powerfully on its first outing? Here is a useful list of stain treatments for unfortunate accidents but, first, a Brummell story about a clumsy accident, related by his first biographer, Captain Jesse. One day, when exiled in France, Brummell was lunching with a young lady when he accidentally spilled a glass of wine on the table. Summoning the waiter, he told him that his companion had caused the mess. When the waiter withdrew, the young lady protested and Brummell told her that he was very sorry for attributing the blame to her but added 'You know it would never have done to let the world know that *I* was guilty of such awkwardness.'

One general point that I must make is that natural fibres, especially wool, often contain natural oils such as lanolin and it is surprising how some natural fabrics will sometimes allow you just to brush off a spillage. Therefore, if you spill some liquid on your trousers look to see whether the oils in the material cause the spilt liquid to congregate in little bubbles. If so, just try brushing the spillage off (avoiding your wife or neighbour, obviously).

Red wine

Immediately apply and gently rub in as much finely ground table salt as possible and then soak in *cold* water. Generally avoid hot water in stain removal because hot water tends to fix the dyeing agent in the material.

Candle wax

Christmas church services frequently have candles burning all over the place and it is all too easy to get the wax on coats, hats, gloves and scarves – causing one fully to appreciate John Donne's words: 'I neglect God and his Angels for the noise of a fly, for the rattling of a coach, for the whining of a door'.

The way to deal with candle wax is to let it dry and scrape off as much as possible with a spoon. Then sandwich the material between sheets of either brown paper or blotting paper and pass a hot iron over the side with most wax on it. Keep moving the paper around so that you are using clean paper each time you iron. Eventually the paper will absorb all the wax.

Bloodstains

Just soak the item in cold water as quickly as possible.

Lipstick

Risk no hostage to fortune – and destroy the affected item at once. Alternatively, dab with diluted hydrogen peroxide.

Scent

Rub the item with a solution of hydrogen peroxide – but be careful to test a hidden portion of cloth first.

Mud

Allow the clothing to dry and then brush off the mud with a stiff brush.

Inks

For fountain pen ink, soak the item in milk for a day and then rinse through with cold water. For biro ink, dab the item with pure alcohol.

Grass

Again, dab this with pure alcohol.

Gravy and sauces

These stains present one of the occasions when warm water and soap can be used to good effect – as a grease-buster.

Coffee

Coat the item in glycerine and rinse off.

Chocolate

First of all, scrape off as much as you can with a spoon and rinse the material in cold water. Apply some liquid detergent for five minutes, add more cold water and rub the stain and rinse.

Chewing gum

Freeze the gum and then crack and crumble it off.

The use of white vinegar

White vinegar is an extremely useful general cleaner and I use it especially to remove marks from my Panama hat (which is now 24 years old and still going strong). It is also especially effective against tea stains.

Tropical mildew

If you decide to live in, or visit a tropical place, be aware at the outset that tropical mildew can be a real problem – especially on leather – and you could open your wardrobe one day to find everything indelibly stained with black spots and streaks of this terrible stuff. However, there are various dehumidifying products available in the supermarkets in tropical countries, which soak up the moist air in which mildew thrives.

Bibliography

BOOKS

Arlott, John, *The Snuff Shop* (Michael Joseph, 1974).

Brewer, E.C., *Brewer's Dictionary of Phrase and Fable* (Cassell & Co, rev. edn 1894).

Barrow, Kenneth, *Mr Chips: The Life of Robert Donat* (Methuen, 1985).

Brimley Johnson, R. (ed.), *Manners Makyth Man* (A.M. Philpot, 1932).

Brittain, F., *Arthur Quiller-Couch: A Biographical Study of Q* (Cambridge University Press, 1947).

Brittain, F., *Q Anthology* (J.M. Dent & Sons, 1948).

Campbell, John, *F.E. Smith, 1st Earl of Birkenhead* (Jonathan Cape, 1983).

Churchill, Winston S., *His Father's Son: The Life of Randolph Churchill* (Weidenfield & Nicolson, 1996).

Cliff, Kenneth, *Mr Lock: Hatter to Lord Nelson and his Norfolk Neighbours* (Wendy Webb Books, 2000).

Coombes, David, *A Careless Rage for Life: Dorothy L Sayers* (Lion, 1992).

Coombes, Joan, *A Fowey Jigsaw Puzzle* (Royal Fowey Yacht Club, 2000).

Cooper, Artemis, *Diana Cooper's Scrap Book* (Hamish Hamilton, 1987).

Davie, Michael (ed.), *Diaries of Evelyn Waugh* (Weidenfield & Nicolson, 1976).

Dobbs, Brian, *The Last shall be First* (Elm Tree Books, 1972).

Duke of Windsor, HRH the, *A Family Album* (Cassell & Co, 1960).

Du Maurier, Daphne, *Gerald: A Portrait* (Victor Gollancz, 1934).

Du Maurier, Georges, *The Novels of Georges du Maurier* (Pilot Press, 1948).

Earl of Birkenhead, *F.E. Smith, 1st Earl of Birkenhead*, by his son (Eyre & Spottiswoode, 1959).

Encyclopaedia Britannica, 15th edn 1985.

Everett, Susanne, *London: The Glamour Years 1919–1939* (Popular Culture Inc., 1985).

Farwell, Byron, *The Life of Sir Richard Francis Burton* (Longmans, Green & Co, 1963).

Fielding, Daphne, *The Duchess of Jermyn Street* (Eyre & Spottiswoode, 1964).

Fitzgerald, Edward, *Rubaiyat of Omar Khayyam*, ed. George F. Maine (Collins, 1953).

Forster, Margaret, *Daphne du Maurier* (Chatto & Windus, 1993).

Galsworthy, John, *The Forsyte Saga: A Modern Comedy* (Heinemann/Octopus (reprint) 1976).

Grosskurth, Phyllis, *Byron: The Flawed Angel* (Hodder & Stoughton, 1997).

Haggard, Lilias, *The Cloak that I Left: The Life of Sir H Rider Haggard* (Hodder & Stoughton, 1951).

Harrison, E., *Scottish Estate Tweeds* (Johnston's of Elgin, 1995).

Hemingway, Ernest, *Death in the Afternoon* (Jonathan Cape, 1932).

Hibbert, Chris, *Nelson: A Personal Portrait* (Penguin, 1994).

Hillyard, Paul, *The Book of the Spider: From Arachnophobia to the Love of Spiders* (Hutchinson, 1994).

Jesse, William, *The Life of George Brummell, Esq.* (Saunders & Otley, 1844).

Leider, Emily W., *Dark Lover: The Life and Death of Rudolph Valentino* (Faber & Faber (reprint) 2004).

Lesley, Cole, *Noel Coward* (Jonathan Cape, 1976).

Lycett, Andrew, *Ian Fleming* (Weidenfeld & Nicolson, 1995).

McCann, Graham, *Cary Grant: A Class Apart* (Fourth Estate, 1997).

Marshall, Michael, *Top Hat and Tails: The Story of Jack Buchanan* (Elm Tree Books, 1978).

Matthews, Roy T. and Peter Mellini, *In Vanity Fair* (Scolar Press, 1982).

Mitford, Nancy, *Noblesse Oblige* (Oxford University Press, 1956).

Morgan, John, *Debrett's New Guide to Etiquette and Modern Manners* (Headline Publishing, 1996).

Morley, Sheridan, *A Talent to Amuse: A Biography of Noel Coward* (Heinemann, 1969).

Morley, Sheridan, *Gladys Cooper: A Biography* (Heinemann, 1979).

Murray, K.M. Elisabeth, *Caught in a Web of Words: James Murray and the Oxford English Dictionary* (Oxford University Press, 1977).

Norman, Barry, *The Hollywood Greats* (Hodder & Stoughton, 1979).

Orczy, Baroness, *Links in the Chain of Life* (Hutchinson, 1971).

Oxford Dictionary of National Biography (Oxford University Press).

Quiller-Couch, Arthur, *On the Art of Writing, the lecture 'On Style'* (Cambridge University Press, 1919).

Rowse, A.L., *Memories and Glimpses* (Methuen, 1986).

Rowse, A.L., *A Portrait of Q* (Methuen, 1988).

Skinner, Cornelia Otis, *Elegant Wits and Grand Horizontals* (Michael Joseph, 1964).

Stevenson, William, *A Man Called Intrepid* (Harcourt, 1976).

Taylor, S.J., *Great Outsiders: Northcliffe, Rothermere and the Daily Mail* (Orion, 1996).

Thomas, J.A.C., *Text Book of Roman Law* (North-Holland Publishing Co., 1976).

Thornton, J.P., *The Sectional System of Gentleman's Garment Cutting, Comprising Coats, Vests, Breeches and Trousers* (Minster & Co, 1894, enlarged 2nd edn).

Titman, G.A., *Dress and Insignia Worn at His Majesty's Court, issued with the authority of the Lord Chamberlain* (Harrison & Sons, 1937).

Treglown, Jeremy, *Roald Dahl* (Farrar, Straus & Giroux, 1994).

Waddy, H.T., *The Devonshire Club and 'Crockford's'* (Eveleigh Nash, 1919).

Walker, Richard, *The Savile Row Story: An Illustrated History* (Tiger Books, 1988).

Wedgewood, C.V., *The Trial of Charles I* (Penguin, 1964).

Weinreb, Ben, and Chris Hibbert, *London Encyclopaedia* (Macmillan, 1983).

Whitbourn, Frank, *Mr Lock of St James's Street* (Heinemann, 1971).

Wodehouse, P.G., *Right-ho! Jeeves* (Herbert Jenkins, 1934).

Wright, F.A., *Lempriere's Classical Dictionary* (Routledge & Kegan Paul, new edn 1949).

PERIODICALS AND MISCELLANEOUS

Army & Navy Stores' Catalogue, 1939.
House of Commons Fact Sheet G7.
London Gazette, 7 May 1920.
London Life, 7 April 1934.
Pall Mall Gazette (various).
The Sunday Times (business section), 9 July 2006.
The Times, 5 December 1837, 21 October 1962.
Time magazine, 18 June 1934.

INTERNET RESOURCES

www.anderson-sheppard.co.uk
www.bristolcars.co.uk
www.classiccars.com
www.cordings.com
www.daks.com
www.daviesandsonsavilerow.com
www.degeskinner.co.uk
www.edeandravenscroft.co.uk
www.florislondon.com
www.gjcleverley.co.uk
www.henrymaxwell.com
www.henrypoole.com
www.hilditchandkey.co.uk
www.johnlobbltd.co.uk
www.lockhatters.co.uk
www.james-smith.co.uk
www.johnstonscashmere.com
www.kilgour.co.uk
www.newandlingwood.com
www.nortonandsons.co.uk
www.pateyhats.com
www.sharrowmills.com
www.swaineadeney.co.uk
www.thechap.net
www.thelondonlounge.net
www.thomasmahon.co.uk
www.thomaspink.com
www.turnbullandasser.co.uk
www.wsfoster.com
www.8savilerow.com

Acknowledgements and Permissions

For permission to reproduce literary works, I am grateful to Cambridge University Press for permission to reproduce, in Chapter 8, the extract from the late Professor Sir Arthur Quiller-Couch's published lecture 'On Style', originally delivered in Cambridge on 28 January 1914 and, subsequently, published in *On the Art of Writing* (1919).

For photographs and illustrations (and necessary permissions to reproduce them), I am grateful to the following:

Getty Images, pages 12, 16, 58, 62, 93 95, 102.

Rex Features, pages 42, 51, 52, 60, 66, 67, 82, 86, 98.

John Wilkes, of The Original Vanity Fair Cartoon Company, for providing the Spy (Sir Leslie Ward) cartoons from Vanity Fair, cover illustrations and pages 33, 73, 76, 80, 121, 165, 166, 169, 170, 172.

My father for his help with checking images, as well as providing that at page 78.

Bookends and Mr and Mrs Coombs, of Fowey and A. G. Williams, Commodore of the Royal Fowey Yacht Club for the photograph of the late Sir Arthur Quiller-Couch, page 148

George Glasgow, of George Cleverley, boot makers, pages 67, 106, 113.

The Honourable Artemis Cooper, for the photograph of her grandfather, Alfred Duff Cooper (1st Viscount Norwich), page 98.

Marie Guilloteau, of Alfred Dunhill, page 34.

Richard Edgecliffe-Johnson, of W. S. Foster & Son and Henry Maxwell, pages 65, 70, 107, 111 (photograph also by courtesy of the photographer, Wolf Media), 127, 128.

Angus Cundey, of Henry Poole, page 97 and for much valuable information from the fir

m's records.

Emma Willis, page 20.

Patrick Grant, of Norton & Sons, pages 47, 90, 118, 122 and for giving permission for the photographs on pages 119 and 124 to be taken by Kenneth Lim.

Kenneth Lim, 7, 100, 101, 109 the latter group (apart from the photograph of the statue of Beau Brummell) taken, by arrangement with Mr Rowley and with the kind permission of Sarah Webster, of Budd Shirt makers.

Janet Taylor, of hatter James Lock & Co, pages 138, 139, 140, 141, 142, 143, 144, 145, 147 and for a wealth of information.

Dr Kenneth Cliff, part-time archivist of the records and family member of James Lock & Co pages 132 and 133 (the former, copyright of James Lock & Co).

Rowland Lowe-MacKenzie, of Turnbull & Asser, pages 24, 107.

Guy Pullen of Clifton Nurseries, page 162

The Metropolitan Museum of Art in New York, page 88 (the articles of clothing represented having been the gift of the Duchess of Windsor).

Justin Sumrie and Sarah Roper, of New & Lingwood, page 24.

Pickett, page 35.

James Smith & Son, page 158.

Johnston's of Elgin, page 44.

I would also like to thank everyone for kindly providing images which, unfortunately, we were not able to use.

I would also like to thank Mr William (Bill) Matthews, formerly of Davies & Son, for much information and advice over the years, Gerald Bladen, manager of Ede & Ravenscroft; Michael Smith (head cutter) and Andrew Skillen, of the tailors Kilgour and Bernard Weatherill; all at Connock & Lockie; the Press Office of tailors and outfitters Gieves & Hawkes. I thank Rina Prentice of the National Maritime Museum and Dr Julian Critchlow and Laurence Mann for their helpful and constructive criticism, along the way. I thank Cornerstone's for their advice; my agent, Andrew Lownie (who went much beyond the call of duty to bring this to life) and his readers, for their help and encouragement, as well as my Commissioning Editor, Fiona Shoop and my Copy Editor, Jane Robson, together with the whole team at Remember When.

Of course, I am grateful to members of my family.

The sub-title of this book originally appeared as the title of an article which Bertie Wooster was commissioned to 'write' for his Aunt Dahlia's magazine, *Milady's Boudoir,* in *Right-ho! Jeeves.*

Where existing craftsmen and their businesses which are mentioned in the text have websites (listed in the Bibliography), I have made use of some of the information to be found there, such as the names of former customers whom they claim; although I have been careful to observe the line between using the information and breaching copyright. Where existing suppliers of goods are mentioned, their contact details are given at the end of the book.

Finally, the views and opinions expressed in this book are my own and just because others have been relied upon as sources of information or illustration does not mean that they are responsible for any errors in this work or that they necessarily hold any of the opinions (whether sartorial or political), which I voice.

Nicholas Storey,
Estado do Rio de Janeiro,
Brasil.

Index of Firms

These appear in alphabetical order, according to the first name or letter of each firm:

A.J. Hewitt (tailor), 9 Savile Row, London W1S 3PF (tel. 0207 734 1505).

Alfred Dunhill (outfitters), 50 Jermyn Street, London SW1Y 6DL (tel. 0207 290 8606).

Anderson & Sheppard (tailors), 32 Old Burlington Street, London W1S 3AT (tel. 0207 734 1620).

Ballantyne Cashmere Shop, 153A New Bond Street, London W1S 2TZ (tel. 0207 495 6184).

Benson & Clegg (tailors, tie suppliers), 9 Piccadilly Arcade, London SW1Y 6NH (tel. 0207 491 1454).

Berk (slippers and woollens), 6 Burlington Arcade, London W1 (tel. 0207 493 1430).

Berluti (shoes), 43 Conduit Street, London W1 (tel. 0207 437 1740).

Bernard Weatherill (tailors), 8 Savile Row, London W1S 3PE (tel. 0207 734 6905).

Berry Brothers & Rudd (wine merchants), 3 St James's Street, London SW1A 1EG (tel. 0207 396 9600).

Borsalino (felt hats), at James Lock & Co and at Herbert Johnson.

Brioni (suiting), 32 Bruton Street, London W1J 6LF (tel. 0207 491 7700).

Bristol Cars Ltd (motor cars), 368–370 Kensington High Street, London W14 8NL (tel. 0207 603 5554).

Brooks Bros (shirts), Old Broad Street, London EC2N 1DW (tel. 0207 256 6013).

Buck's Club, 18 Clifford Street, London W1S 3RF (tel. 0207 734 9896).

Budd Shirtmakers, 1a–3 Piccadilly Arcade, London SW1Y 6NH (tel. 0207 493 0139).

Burberry (rain wear), 165 Regent Street, London W1B 4PH (tel. 0207 734 4060).

Campbell's (tweed makers), The Highland Tweed House, Beauly, Inverness-shire IV4 7BU (tel. 01463 782239).

Cavendish Hotel, 81 Jermyn Street, London SW1Y 6JF (tel. 0207 930 2111).

Charvet (ties), 28 Place Vendome, 75001 Paris (tel. 33 142 962707).

Chester Barrie (suiting), 18–19 Savile Row, London W1S 3PP (tel. 0207 439 6079).

Church's (shoes), For nearest stockist, call 01604 593333.

Clifton Nurseries (plants), 5A Clifton Villas, London W9 2 PH (tel. 0207 289 6851).

Connock & Lockie Ltd (tailors), 33 Lamb's Conduit Street, London WC1N 3NG (tel. 0207 831 2479).

Cording's (country gear), 19 Piccadilly, London W1V 0PE (tel. 0207 734 0830).

Costello & Sons (tailors), 284-294 Ley Street, Ilford, Essex IG1 4BS (tel. 0208 478 2780).

Crockett & Jones (shoes), 20–21 Burlington Arcade, London W1V 9AF (tel. 0207 499 6676).

Czeck & Speake (for cologne), 39c Jermyn Street, London SW1Y 6DN (tel. 0207 439 0216).

Daks (outfitters), 101 Jermyn Street, SW1Y 6EE (tel. 0207 409 4000).

Davies & Son (London) Ltd (tailors), 38 Saville Row, London W1S 3QE (tel. 0207 437 7986).

Dege & Skinner (tailors), 10 Savile Row, London W1S 3PF (tel. 0207 287 2941).

Douglas Hayward (tailor), 95 Mount Street, London W1 (tel. 0207 499 5574).

Dormeuil (cloths), through your tailor.

Ede & Ravenscroft (tailors, robemakers and outfitters), 93 Chancery lane, London WC2A 1DU (tel. 0207 405 3906).

Edward Green & Co (shoes), 12–13 Burlington Arcade, London W1V 9AB (tel. 0207 499 6377).

Emma Willis (shirt-maker and hosier), 66 Jermyn Street, London SW1Y 6NY (tel. 0207 930 9980).

Evisu (bespoke jeans), 9 Savile Row, London W1S 3PF (tel. 0207 734 2540).

Farlow's (fishing tackle and waders), 9 Pall Mall, London SW1Y 5NP (tel. 0207 484 1000).

Gaziano & Girling (shoemakers), 3 Harding Close, Kettering, Northants NN15 5DQ (tel. 01536 511022).

Gieves & Hawkes (tailors and outfitters), 1 Savile Row, London W1S 3JR (tel. 0207 434 2001).

G.J. Cleverley & Co (bespoke and readymade slippers, shoes and boots), 13 Royal Arcade, 28 Old Bond Street, London W1S 4SL (tel. 0207 493 0443).

G. Smith & Son (cigars and snuffs), 74 Charing Cross Road, London WC2H 0BG (tel. 0207 836 7422).

Grenson (shoes), tel. 01933 354300.

G. Trumper (colognes and barbers), 9 Curzon Street, London W1J 5HQ (tel. 0207 499 1850).

Hackett (outfitters), 87 Jermyn Street, London SW1Y 6JD (tel. 0207 930 1300).

Hardy Amies (designers and tailors), 14 Savile Row, London W1S 3JN (tel. 0207 734 2436).

Harrods', 81–135 Brompton Road, London SW1X 7XL (tel. 0207 730 1234).

Harvie & Hudson (shirts, ties, chuddies and cords), 96-97 Jermyn Street, London SW1Y 6JE (tel. 0207 839 3578).

Hawes & Curtis (shirts), 23 Jermyn Street, London SW1Y 6HP (tel. 0207 287 8111).

Henry Maxwell, see W.S. Foster & Son.

Henry Poole (tailor), 15 Saville Row, London W1S 3PJ (tel. 0207 734 5985).

Herbert Johnson (hats), 54 St James's Street, London SW1A 1JT (tel. 0207 408 1174).

Hermes (ties), 155 New Bond Street, London W1S 2UA (tel. 0207 499 8856).

Hetherington Hats, 25A Walpole Street, London SW3 4QS (tel. 0207 730 2948).

Hilditch & Key (shirts and ties), 73 Jermyn Street, London SW1Y 6NP (tel. 0207 930 5336).

Holland & Sherry (cloths), 9–10 Savile Row, London W1S 3PF (tel. 0207 437 0404).

Hunter Sovereign (wellies) available at Cording's.

H. Huntsman & Sons (tailors), 11 Savile Row, London W1S 3PS (tel. 0207 734 7441).

Irish Linen Company (linens), 35–36 Burlington Arcade, London W1J 0QB (tel. 0207 493 8949).

James Lock & Co (hats), 6 St James's Street, London SW1A 1EF (tel. 0207 930 8874).

James Smith & Sons (umbrellas and sticks), 53 New Oxford Street, London WC1A 1BL (tel. 0207 836 4731).

James Taylor & Son (bespoke shoes), 4 Paddington Street, London W1U 5QE (tel. 0207 935 4149).

J. Barbour & Sons (waxed country coats), at Cording's.

J. Floris (colognes), 89 Jermyn Street, London SW1Y 6JH (tel. 0845 702 3239).

John B. Stetson Hat Company, www.stetson.com

John Lobb Ltd (bespoke slippers, shoes and boots), 9 St James' Street, London SW1A 1EF (tel. 0207 930 3664).

John Smedley (cotton tops), 19 King's Road, London SW3 4RP (tel. 0207 823 4444).

Johnston's of Elgin (tweed makers), Cashmere Visitor Centre, Newmill, Elgin, Morayshire IV30 2AF (tel. 01343 554099).

Kilgour (tailors), 8 Savile Row, London W1S 3PF (tel. 0207 734 6905).

Laurence Corner (second-hand gear, including sola topees), 62 Hampstead Road, London NW1 2NU (tel. 0207 813 1010).

Laszlo Vass (shoe-maker), Andrew Harris e-mail: andrew@vass-shoes.com

Le Chameau (wellies), Carlo Beretta House, 11 Brunel Way, Fareham, Hants PO15 5TX (tel. 01489 579999).

Les Senteurs (colognes), 71 Elizabeth Street, London SW1W 9PJ (tel. 0207 730 2322).

Lewins (shirts, ties and chuddies), 106 Jermyn Street, London SW1Y 6EQ (tel. 0207 930 4291).

Loden (capes), www.born-for-loden.co.uk

Loro Piana, 153 New Bond Street, London W1 (tel. 0207 499 9300).

Mayfair Laundry, Stirling Road, London W3 (tel. 0208 992 3041).

McBean's Orchids, sales@mcbeansorchids.co.uk

Meyer & Mortimer Ltd (tailors), 6 Sackville Street, London W1S 3DD (tel. 0207 734 3135).

Michael German (old sticks and canes), 38b Kensington Church Street, London W8 4BX (tel. 0207 937 2771).

N Peal (jumpers), 71–72 Burlington Arcade, London W1 (tel. 0207 493 5376).

New & Lingwood (shoes, shirts, chuddies, ties and socks), 53 Jermyn Street, London SW1Y 6LX (tel. 0207 499 5340).

Norton & Sons (tailors), 16 Savile Row, London W1S 3PL (tel. 0207 437 0829).

Oliver Brown (outfitters), 75 Lower Sloane Street, London SW1W 8DA (tel. 0207 259 9494).

Ozwald Boateng (tailor), 9 Vigo St, London W1X 1AL (tel. 0207 437 0620).

Patey Hats (bespoke hats), 9 Gowlett Road, Dulwich, London SE15 4HZ (tel. 0207 635 0030).

Paul Davies (shoemaker), tel. 01795 427694.

Pickett (gloves), 32–33 Burlington Arcade, London W1V 9AE (tel. 0207 493 8936).

Richard James (tailor), 29 Savile Row, London W1S 3PY (tel. 0207 434 0605).

Scabal (cloths), through your tailor.

Steven Hitchcock (tailor), 13 New Bond Street, London W1 S 3BG (tel. 0207 287 2492).

Swaine Adeney Brigg (umbrellas and riding accessories), 54 St James' Street, London SW1A 1JT (tel. 0207 409 7277).

Taylor of Old Bond Street (colognes), 74 Jermyn Street, London SW1Y 6NP (tel. 0207 930 5544).

Timothy Everest (tailor), B/24 Corbet Place, London E1 6NH (tel. 0207 426 4883).

Thomas Mahon (tailor), e-mail: info@thomasmahon.co.uk

Thomas Pink (shirts), 85 Jermyn Street, London SW1Y 6JD (tel. 0207 498 3882).

Tricker's (R.E.) (shoes), 67 Jermyn Street, London SW1Y 6NY (tel. 0207 930 6395).

Turnbull & Asser (shirts and ties), 71–72 Jermyn Street, London SW1Y 6PF (tel. 0207 808 3000).

Wain Shiell (cloths), through your tailor.

Washington Tremlett (shirts and ties), at Kilgours, 8 Saville Row, London W1S 3PE (tel. 0207 734 6905).

W. Bill (cloths), through your tailor.

Welsh & Jeffries (tailors), 20 Savile Row, London W1S 3PR (tel. 0207 734 3062).

Wilson's of Sharrow (snuff chandlers), Through G. Smith & Sons.

W.S. Foster & Son (bespoke slippers, shoes and boots), 83 Jermyn Street, London SW1 (tel. 0207 930 5385).

Yves St Laurent (designer), 171–172 Sloane Street, London SW1X 9QG (tel. 0207 235 6706).

General index